MUSIC HISTORY IN LAYERS

ITS EUROPEAN CONTINUUM

MICHAEL G. CUNNINGHAM

authorHOUSE®

AuthorHouse™
1663 Liberty Drive
Bloomington, IN 47403
www.authorhouse.com
Phone: 1 (800) 839-8640

Published by AuthorHouse   10/23/2015

ISBN: 978-1-5049-5752-6 (sc)
ISBN: 978-1-5049-5753-3 (e)

Library of Congress Control Number: 2015917511

Print information available on the last page.

Any people depicted in stock imagery provided by Thinkstock are models, and such images are being used for illustrative purposes only. Certain stock imagery © Thinkstock.

This book is printed on acid-free paper.

LAYER I for rank beginners, Freshmen music majors and informed casual readers.

LAYERS I and II for Music Professionals, Sophomore Music Majors, and those who will not use, nor benefit from excessive mini-details.

LAYER III relies on existing Music History books.

TABLE OF CONTENTS

Preface

As the title page says, this book is intended for at least two types of individuals, those wishing to know Music History in only the barest essentials, and those who need some orientation before beginning intensive study. It is not intended solely as a College book, but rather also for the many music enthusiasts outside of Academia. How knowledge of this subject serves you in your chosen field determines how much you need to know. This book recognizes that and offers appropriate information for two levels of need.

Music Majors, it seems, frequently need some sort of preliminary exposure to Music History before enrolling in a course so-named. Even professors of the subject, often taught in the third year of Baccalaureate degrees, prefer having students with more orientation than the small snippets gained in early Theory and Music Appreciation Courses.

A review of Music History need not mention all composers who have entered the common repertory. Some readers may feel cheated if their favorite composers are either downplayed or omitted. That is a false worry. Historic overviews must dwell on and highlight salient people and techniques as time passes. It may be that the best music, or at least the best of outstanding scores were created by a singular figure not in the mainstream of salient developments. So, by all means, the reader is encouraged to stay with his or her original tastes and beliefs.

Here birth and death dates of specific composers are downplayed. Rather, periods of influence and accomplishments are more important. There are also practically no listening recommendations. It is a separate, but important area of development for the reader, on each's own, to hear what all the historic talk is about. Yes, this book makes all the more sense when coordinated music is heard and known, and (contrarily) yes, one could digest all that is here without ever hearing any of the music involved. That second point is the option of the reader.

Special thanks to colleague Prof. Paul Hilbrich for reading the manuscript.

M.G.C.

LAYER I

ANCIENT TIMES

In Pre--Christian Greek Culture music was sung and played on crudely created flute and harp--type instruments. Pipes with holes, and stretched gut--strings could produce pitches that matched the notes of singers. Such instruments were really inherited from the earlier cultures of nearby Asia Minor. This earliest occidental music would be intrinsically linked with textual content. Specific names of the early Occidental instruments are unimportant at this point, as long as the reader understands their link with the basic first appearances of organized music. The linked solo sung texts would serve all manner of functions: religion, superstition, sports, ceremonies, monarchy, etc.

The ancient/Classical Greeks would forever remain rational, word--literate, systematic, and before the Christian Era would eventually develop various changing explanations concerning the note--level mechanics of music. Over time these explanations would also be forever changing. The later Christian musicians in their day would benefit from these ancient writings in very general ways.

That was about the extent of music in the Classic Greek, and even Roman periods,------right up to, and beyond the start of the Christian era. Going on from there, and broadly speaking, the years 500 to 1000 in the West were centuries filled with rampant chaos, illiteracy and violent upheaval. Even by 1000 and beyond, roving bands of pillagers were still on the move.

THE EARLIEST CHRISTIAN ERA (50 – 600 Common Era)

At first Christianity was an underground religious movement (50 – 312). During this time the Church organized itself and took stock of its group and solo singing of hymns and other sacred texts. Eventually that practice was to become common. After the legalization of Christianity in 312, the practice of such singing became common to Christian worship. The music of Constantinople was easily more advanced than that of Rome, and that capitol of the Christian Roman Empire of the East benefited from the practices of nearby Asia Minor. The musical chanting typical of the disbursed Jewish groups was particularly influential. So far as is known, music in the Christian church would remain monophonic (single melody) until around 800. And the melodies attached to sacred texts would be passed from generation to generation by musical memorization. That process seems to have been remarkably accurate.

At first Constantinople would have a culture that was a blend Greek and Latin elements. In time the Greek and Eastern religious elements would win out. Eventually the Roman Empire, and its religious stylistic practices split from the East. There would be a permanent cultural (and musical) division. But in both centers the chanting of sacred texts would be common, but different. Considering the chaos that the West would endure, its own Chant eventually materialized, but where did it come from? It had to have been influenced by the Greek Chant of Constantinople, but to what extent? Scholars in more recent times have had limited success in matching specific melodies in both differing cultures.

600 ----800

So it was that during this period that Gregorian Chant (named after an organizing pope—Gregory I, Papacy 590 -- 604) emerged as the dominant form of Western Christian music. Gregorian Chant organization apparently resulted in the organizing, standardizing, and codifying substantial collections of sacred chant melodies gathered from the diverse Christian enclaves around the Mediterranean. This task would be made somewhat difficult because of the lack of a written music notation. But at the time, the existing church scholar/ musicians saw to it that all melodies conformed to and fitted into eight possible mode/ scales. Modes here meant not just scales, but also melodic mannerisms.

800 ---- 1000

Around 800, during the Carolingian/Charlemagne period, there was a brief cultural reawakening, when even ink was rediscovered. It was also the period when all realized a strong central monarchy could protect its citizens. At last there was some form of security. And in attempting to standardize its chant melodies in the above--mentioned period there now led to a form of written notation involving pitches only. At first the attempts were crude and lacking in clarity, but in time after 1000 a stave gradually evolved and progress was being made. At about 800 there were steps towards a crude form of harmony brought about by the singing of multiple simultaneous voices in parallel motion.

The Church did not recognize or preserve secular music, even though it obviously existed. Considering the instable and turbulent times, there were times when even sacred music survived by a slim thread.

1000 – 1200

As the new millennium began in 1000, examples of a crudely notated music appear on stretched animal skin (parchment). Cultured behavior, along with improved musical practices were taking place in castles, towns and cities, and especially in Paris. The first of the Crusades began, which in turn led to travelers returning from Asia Minor with cultural ideas. These two hundred years would see positive music developments, almost becoming too numerous to mention. Among them would be success in recording Gregorian Chant in a readable notation on a stave. This was a momentous step forward. This era would see a burgeoning European economy, the formation of towns, and the construction of massively tall Gothic Cathedrals.

Systematized teaching of church singers would continue. Along with this teaching was the need for clarity of scale labeling, and melodic methodology. Some of the scale labeling (A through G, ut through la) would lead to our modern way of thinking. Though monophonic chanting would continue, church music in select enclaves would be progressively contrapuntal with multiple simultaneous voices, and a growing need for better control of rhythm.

There would be a glimmer of recognition of secular music. Certain castles and civilized settlements/districts played host to traveling minstrel singers and performers. Those transients performed what is thought to be a single line music that could easily be quite spare in, if not devoid of religious textual content. Secular music of this type was quite typical in Occitania, certain southern provinces of France. In the 1100s, Occitanian aristocratic author/composers were called Troubadours, and would produce poems and songs that usually extolled life's pleasures and the complications of love. The Occitanian culture would be ruthlessly eliminated in the early 1200s. The surviving songs, only preserved in melodic form, probably involved a rhythmic continuum of compound beats (like the very basic rhythms possible in half of a 6/8 measure).

1200s ---- THE NOTRE DAME SCHOOL

From the accounts, this seems to have been a successful century, especially in music. In the 1200s most of the important music developments took place in France, and specifically in Paris. Adding to the success was that (almost) political extension of France known now as England. Both monarchies were united by the French language and by dynastic intertwining overlordships. Moreover, since the two monarchies were in positions of strength, for the time being war was kept to a minimum. Progress was in the air, no doubt aided the newly built cathedrals that remained standing. They were a testament to man's ability. The Magna Carta was signed in 1215.

Ground was gained in the development of polyphony/harmony in liturgical music. In the act of combining several differing lines of music simultaneously, the rhythmic control of each voice became mandatory. The Parisian minds of the day came up with the so--called SIX RHYTHMIC MODES. These were six mental templates (in our present day 6/8 and 9/8 meters) that each singer would use in reading non--rhythmic notation in their separate parts. Each new phrase in the music might be in one of the Rhythmic Modes.

Secular monophonic song would continue strong because the northern reaches of France had its share of aristocratic love song composers called Trouveres. These northerners could not help but remember in anxiety what had happened to their Southern brethren, the Troubadours, and how they had been wiped out in Occitania in 1209, or so. The love song creation continued.

The polyphony/harmony in the religious music of the 1200s and even the coming 1300s involved the basic intervals perfect 5ths and octaves. There would always be an "adaptation" of a melody from the liturgy that was the main musical line to include in any new piece. If two or three simultaneous voices moved about independently, all manner of "white--key" dissonances could result between the heart--speed beats, provided there were perfect 5ths, unisons and octaves on the beat. The earliest kind of polyphony had several names: the most prominent of which was Organum. Other labels were Discant, Conductus, and Motet. The 1200s Motet always involved a brief textual line in an early form of French. Texts could easily refer to Eternity and other meanings loosely connected to the meaning of the liturgical line. Important composers of the 1200s were "Anonymous," Leonin and Perotin in Paris, and Petrus de Cruce in Italy. Petrus, associated with an Italian manner of notation, was apparently born in France.

THE 1300s

The 1300s were troubled times, there being two appearances of the Black Plague and the seemingly endless dynastic wars over the English Platagenet lands in France and the French throne.

THE FOUR PROLATIONS (metric schemes)

This century is referred to as the Ars Nova, meaning New Art, and so named because of a famous treatise by the same name, written by Philippe de Vitry early in the century. This treatise was an official endorsement of a new way of handling rhythm: THE FOUR PROLATIONS. This approach had replaced the older RHYTHMIC MODES. Though there would be no bar lines in music until the l600s, the new method, in its own way, would allow for the heartbeat speed of beats to be formatted into two kinds of duple meter, and two kinds of triple. Beat partials in turn could be formatted into duple and triple groupings. (Simple beat, versus the compound beat). In broad, general modern terms, it allowed for 2/4, 6/8, 3/4 and 9/8. Once again the performer would be required to read from a seemingly generic line of music, while reading into it a metric template. That means the same line could possibly be demonstrably read successively in any of the four meters.

Thus an additional Ars Nova innovation was the very acceptance of the duple and quadruple meters. Formerly music was fixated on metric groups of threes and its implied connection with the Holy Trinity. Ars Nova music was also a step closer to secular music, and it resulted in perhaps the first competition between music that was beautiful because of its intellectual content, and music that was beautiful because of its intuitive content. (Machaut versus Landini)

A common texture significant for later developments was that of nascent monody (melody and accompaniment). It was the Cantilena/Ballade style that featured a sung melody and an accompaniment of two lines played on lutes and/or string instruments. This style would continue on into the late 1400s. There is something universal about Monody. It would be taken up again in the l600s, and it would remain a standard feature of music.

The 1300s would also see highly developed Isorhythmic motets and Masses. Isorhythm is the same thing that Ostinato would be in later Music History. It is a strand of line that would be statically repeated throughout the motet. Nascent appearances can be traced to music of the previous centuries. And the 1300s would see the technique carried to high technical levels.

Other typical forms were the Mass, religious and ceremonial Motets, and secular Rondel types that involved alternation between A and B sections. Also, music was always linked or accompanied by early, basic string and wind instruments, as well as small, and larger organs. There was probably rarely, if ever, a pure choral sound.

1400 -- 1450

Progress in the development of music would remain primarily in the Choral field. Instrumental music would undoubtedly remain in the "unofficial" background, what with the timeless need for peasants to sing and dance. Also this new century would see the invention of the clavichord and harpsichord. Gregorian Chant would continue in all church music, both as monophonically sung and as "seed" elements in newer contrapuntal works. Hence famous Gregorian melodies would be woven into new musical textures and fabrics. This is also the century when sound of the triad was "discovered" and found its way into all official choral music. Its sound was used without it ever being labeled and focused on as an entity until several centuries later.

The English always preferred the sound of thirds and 6ths in their harmony. They were even the first to employ "twin" parallel voice movement of 3rds and 6ths. The English inaugurated the use of parallel 6th chords at this time. (Although it should be remembered that the theoretical thinking of both triads and figured bass did not yet exist yet for a few centuries.) Also, another likely influence on the music of England came from Italy in Landini's use in his highly popular Cantilena/Ballade style pieces of what would later be called triadic harmony. (There would be an almost inexplicable and undocumented connection between English and Italian music during this period.)

Triads in concentration in English music can first be heard in the early 1400s in the music of John Dunstable. However, his choral pieces avoid dissonance of any type. It is a continuum of pure triads. Dunstable had been living on French soil during the on--going Plantagenet wars for the French throne. Thus his music would have been heard by the contemporaneous northern French, Low--Lander and Burgundian composers.

Before long the continental composers would infuse the constant triadic sound with dissonance created by moving lines. That dissonance took the form of passing tones and suspensions, both of which helped to delineate the rhythmic beats. Suspensions, especially, made the strong metric position beats all the more obvious. Dissonance also helped in artistic expressiveness (tension and release). And the result was mature Renaissance (choral) music.

THE RENAISSANCE (in music) BEGINS 1450 -- 1500

The Humanistic Renaissance probably began as early as the late 1200s, while Music's Renaissance began in the mid 1400s. In present day overview, the chief continental composer was Guillaume Dufay (approx. 1400 to 1475), who by the mid 1400s was creating triadically infused four--voice Renaissance choral works. It was a music almost devoid of imitative lines, that development waiting until the next generation of composers in the later decades of the century. Dufay also took the first step in creating free bass lines to better control harmonic change. Previously the bass line's task of presenting the mandatory Gregorian line was a hindrance.

Thus it was that the whole Renaissance (choral) music movement was ignited by Dunstable's works, and Dufay was at the continental lead. After 1450 the greatest Renaissance choral works would come about as composers followed Dufay's lead. From Dufay and on Choral music would have ubiquitous triads. A contemporary of Dufay's was the Burgundian composer Gilles Binchois who, along with some other lowlander composers, took the Cantilena/Ballade style to its highest possibilities in their Masses and secular Rondel pieces.

It was a time for producing Masses, which in hindsight reflect all the forward tendencies in the music at that time. Many Masses would be in four voices (boy sopranos and altos), a four--voice standard we would later call "familiar style." Each Mass consisted of the parts of the Mass that were heard in every Mass: *Kyrie, Gloria, Sanctus* and *Agnus Dei*. Each Mass movement at this time had its own borrowed Gregorian melody, but usually no particular melody unified all the movements. Any borrowed Chant melody was planned to be recognizable, even with added decorous notes. Some Masses could merely begin four or five sections with only the head of the Gregorian melody. These Masses collectively were called Plainsong (Gregorian melody) Masses, even though some Masses would borrow melodies outside the Chant Canon. This method of Mass creation was firmly in place by 1450 and continued on into the 1500s.

The leading composer during the last part of the century was Josquin des Pres (1440--1521), presently regarded as the composer having the greatest long--term effect. In his day he was regarded as highly important. While most of his life was spent in the late 1400s, he was well ahead of his time in that his music foretold practically all techniques in choral music in the 1500s. His full impact was felt after the publication of his work just after 1500. He and his generation usually wrote in four equal (male) voices, and they added linear imitation to the various methods inherited from Dufay. While having Root movement typically by 2nds, and 3rds, an advanced trait is that his music has conspicuous cadences by 5th. Such Root movement, though not recognized as such at the time, would be the feature in the rapidly advancing Choral Art in the later 1500s. Josquin created 20 Masses, 100 motets and 70 secular pieces. In his latter years he was acclaimed and respected by all his contemporaries.

Important Theoretical writings concerning the methods of writing music appeared. In 1475, the Tinctoris musical "encyclopedia" appeared, a few books of which explained to composers just how to move from triad to triad. (And remember the triad as a label and an entity, apparently was not yet isolated in anyone's mind.) The Tinctoris instruction books explained just how 1500s choral music should be put together, voice by voice and chord by chord. Most of the stated rules can be seen being observed in scores as late as the 1590s.

The 1400s ended with four or five composers, chief of whom was, or course, Josquin des Pres. It may well be that Josquin's greatest period of creativity was over by 1500, but still his achievements, about to come out in print for all to see, were highly influential. It was a period that saw the ascendency of composers from the lands immediatcly northeast of France. Josquin's contemporaries created music that would easily rival his in consistent quality.

Because of the relative stability brought on by the Hapsburg and French Dynasties with their strong central governments and the rampant cultural cross fertilization, significant composers were appearing in England, Germany, Western Europe and Italy. Certainly the Papacy also played a role in the production of top--grade choral music. To be an accepted composer in one of the Hapsburg Catholic seats of power (Rome, Madrid, and the moving capitol of the Holy Roman Empire) meant both music and composer would have a presence in all those locations. In time, some forms of Protestantism would revert to music of a basic plainness, but other than for that, Music on the whole was advancing and thriving considerably.

1500s CHORAL MUSIC IN THE ASCENDENCY

As the year 1500 approached, choral music, the only kind of music that officially mattered at the time, experienced an eminence of achievement and development. Printing of music began in 1501 in Venice, commenced in Paris in 1528, and in England two years later. Maybe the 1500s highpoint in choral music was aided by the excitement in the air caused by the discovery of a New World across the Atlantic, and a little later by the cultural competition brought on by the Protestant movement. But even without a New World or Protestantism, the change to a new century would have brought about new attitudes and plans. It would be a truly new and innovative time, and a highpoint would be reached through the medium of choral music. Except for a few lulls, choral achievements would continue appearing throughout the 1500s.

Midway through the 1500s the Madrigal crystalized, resulting in yet more musical riches for decades to come. As the century continued to its end, Giovanni Pierluigi da Palestrina (1525 – 94) would create a treasury of choral riches that would stay in musicians' minds for centuries to come. Then, almost systematically, the choral bonanza began abating around 1600. It was increasingly out of fashion. But, for the time being, Choral music was supreme.

LEADING UP THE 1600s

The musical situation did not abruptly change in l600. Rather, there were a number of practices, some only seemingly new, that had begun some time before that year. Block--chordal writing with figured bass had been rapidly catching on. Violin and keyboard lines were becoming more elaborate. There were troubles ahead, especially religious ones, but Music would endure and grow even amidst political and religious turmoil.

The 1600s

(Often thought of as the first part of a Baroque stylistic period that ended in 1750.)

Most of the first half of the l600s was plagued by constant, bloody warfare between the many Catholic and Protestant kingdoms in geographical Germany. Intellectual writings increased in spite of Church fear of diversified thinking. The Catholic Church, to offset the marked stark values espoused by certain Protestant groups, decided to emphasize beauty; beauty that would spark appropriate emotion. This aspect of the "Counter--Reformation" led to excessively decorated Catholic church interiors, and that mind--set in turn probably led to excessively decorative music. Hence Baroque music could easily be described as excessive in that sense.

In this century instrumental music came into its own. Inroads were made in thinking and composing. Maybe this development rivals Opera in importance. Formerly texts and poems were all that were necessary to make sense of any musical process. Now, without texts, musical repetition and variation became a necessity. A--B--A forms became all the more necessary and were varied and exploited. Otherwise listeners would have been mystified. Musical rhythm reflected the new advances in Mathematics, so a metrical bar line became essential. Meters were clearly thought out and notes were placed in divisional groupings in various speeds afforded by the meter. Music thus became far more metric than in former centuries. Instruments were also improved, thus giving rise to particularized writing.

It would be a century of refined harmonic progressions, made so because of the prominence of the harpsichord, with music consisting of bass lines with figured bass (short hand chord symbols). In the 1500s chords moved about somewhat randomly, with chordal successions that were unique to each composition. But now chords would change in patterns. Eventually the V – I became common. Even though modal cadences would persist, by the end of the 1600s the Major/minor scale system was fully in place, with significant composers creating works that favored chordal progressions that made the Tonic chord obvious. (Tonality) Though the compositions changed, familiar chordal progressions could be heard being repeated at strategic parts of phrases from work to work.

In the first half of the 1600s famous composers were Monteverdi, Cesti, Caccini, Cavalli, Carissimi and Landi. These were invariably opera composers active in the relatively more peaceful Italy. Outstanding operas are Monteverdi's 1607 *Orfeo*, then later in mid--century Landi's *Saint Alessio*, and Cesti's *The Golden Apple*. Instrumental Music, on the other hand was undergoing a period of experimentation.

OPERA AS AN INDEPENDENT ENTITY.

Choral music would continue in the churches, and to some extent in the stream of operas that were created. The solo human voice would be ever present because of opera and opera--like situations (cantatas and oratorios). Opera would be here to stay, but it would always be an independent entity, and not fully music. In fact, other than for sheer experimentation, music plays only a partial role in any successful opera. It is a medium that is too subject to the whims of non-- or partially-- musical audience members, often there just to evaluate voices. And even further, it is seldom that any quality "stand--alone" music finds itself in any usual opera. If any music seems outstanding, the listener is busy relating and confusing/associating the plot situation with the music, rather than its abstract musical quality. If anything, opera would give to abstract music an emphasis on dramatic effects through the juxtaposition of opposite qualities, and the challenge to depict various emotional states.

An increase of colonial lands, and contact with primitive cultures in the Western Hemisphere influenced some European music. For instance, the Chaconne was probably filtered into Europe through Spain. The Thirty--Years War, ending in 1648, certainly held back musical advances, and for a while there would be few outstanding figures, organist Girolamo Frescobaldi being an exception. In the second half of the century Heinrich Schutz would gain fame both in Italy and Germany. Before the 1600s ended Jean--Baptiste Lully's formalistic operas would entertain the Louis 14 court. Lully's pleasingly formal and stilted music would be highly imitated. In some respects the l600s were a dress rehearsal for the momentous music of the next half--century.

1699: THE SITUATION

While Italian Operas and Cantatas seemed to dominate most of Europe's cultural centers, Instrumental Music was making much headway. Formerly vocal melodies were being played on instruments with much added ornamentation. Now melodies and lines were being conceived directly and idiomatically for instruments. Imitative contrapuntal pieces had developed into the Fugue. Pieces formerly in sections had become Dance and Church Suites (often called Sonatas). The Passacaglia and Chaconne had emerged. Theme and Variations had become common. Improvisations at the keyboard on specific chorale melodies had become the Chorale Prelude. Warm--up pieces for the keyboard or lute had become Preludes and Toccatas. Ways of playing the violin and keyboard solidified into idiomatic patterns. String groups were becoming common and were playing multi--movement sets of pieces. The stage was set for the appearance of a momentous figure.

1700 ----1750 JOHANN SEBASTIAN BACH

The most significant occurrence in this period was the life and accomplishments of J. Sebastian Bach (1685 – 1750). He was fifteen in 1700 and already his approach to harmonic progressions far exceeded that of his accomplished contemporaries of whom there were many. He was also building on the achievements and traditions of his Bach--family predecessors and kin. Of the contemporaneous composers, many would have fame, and would be adept at incorporating in their music surfacy fashionable elements. Most, one might say, were constant in their attention to clear melodic presentation with obvious tunes. The more successful ones could score for vary large groups in arriving at a grandiosity of many voices and instruments busily exciting the listener. In time they would all acknowledge Bach's supremacy at fugal writing, but at the same time they know their approach got the better paying jobs.

Bach, on the other hand, knew that solid music construction depended on beauty achieved in miniature – at the keyboard. If a harmonic continuum could prove interesting or beautiful there, then merely expanding it with many layers and voices would prove timeless. Bach, as was typical of his time, utilized extensive metric divisions. He was also the timeless master of the fugue. Whereas the fugues of his contemporaries presented equal voices, and repeated mottos within a harmonic framework that ranged from predictably routine to flat--out dull, Bach's equal voices ride on a harmonic picture that is progressive and dynamic.

Bach's period is often referred to as the HIGH BAROQUE, and he is most often given shared fame with his exact contemporary, G. F. Handel, the London creator of operas and oratorios, especially the particularly popular oratorio, Messiah. However, it is the music of Sebastian Bach that reigns supreme because of its finely wrought inner mechanics of linear relationships and the overall harmonic picture. All are a joy to hear, and can be demonstrated and verified in miniature score reduction.

Bach could be easily bested in a number of specious ways. Often his lines aim at ideals that ignore play-- or singability. His successful contemporaries could be better at orchestration, better at opera or oratorio, better at obvious melodic or tune content, better at making money, better at contemporary popularity, better at association with powerful monarchs, and especially better at fashionable elements. His more important early contemporaries were Francois Couperin and Archangelo Corelli. In addition to Handel, his famous exact contemporaries would be Antonio Vivaldi, and the important Theorist/composer Jean--Philippe Rameau.

The procedures of TONALITY were coming together and being clarified just as Bach was a teenager. In Bach's music the V – I resolution was insufficient. Rather it was the IV (ii) – V – I progression or cadence that would frame, and buttress most phrases. This indeed made the tonic triad, temporary or permanent, sound all the more clear. In all his music, and especially the fugues, chordal progressions enhancing the tonic triad were apparent. And the progressions could be daring. Contrast that with the music of many of his contemporaries, especially the early ones, that had either overly safe, static, or meandering chordal successions with an occasional V – I thrown in. It is the deftly original and acoustical superior (in the Rameau Theoretical sense) harmonic change, and modulations that make J. Sebastian's music stand out.

Concerning his successful and famous contemporaries: In addition to Handel, who was experiencing many successes in London, Vivaldi and Rameau were having their successes. Antonio Vivaldi frequently toured around the Continent, creating Italian--style operas and string--orchestra-- accompanied concertos for various instruments. He evidently created at lightning speed, and the results, while easily pleasing audiences (then and now) sound glib and repetitious. Too many of his instrumental works sound alike.

If one ignores the Theoretical achievements of Jean Philippe Rameau, what emerges is a composer of a number of operas aimed at the aristocracy and intelligentsia of Paris. Even though he arrived at a unique personal sound in his clear melodic presentation, and in his orchestration and basic harmony, the results add up to the same problem Vivaldi had: Too many of Rameau operas, while sounding impressive, seem too alike.

The fifty--year period (1700--50) produced many composers in addition to the ones described here, and most of them created decent, well--constructed, but plain scores. A problem for the 21st Century is to avoid being overwhelmed by Baroque, and even so--called Preclassic music that is superficially pleasing mainly because it sounds passable and is old. Without a perspective, one could easily get lost in a plethora of mediocrity. Moreover, if such music is constantly played as atmospheric "wallpaper" in homes, restaurants, lobbies and the like, listeners are conditioned to hearing things once without really listening, thus eroding the capacity to recognize true genius when it is heard.

Some other important forms or media that matured during the first half of the 1700s were Oratorio, religious Arias, organ music, organ Chorale Preludes, string ensemble music and the Trio Sonata.

OPERA THROUGHOUT THE 1700s

The 1700s would see a proliferation of opera production and patronage. It was needed entertainment. All important composers wrote operas, including Mozart who, late in the century, created his seven or eight mature ones that continue seeing productions centuries later. Even his youthful operas were getting attention.

To some extent music developed and grew simultaneously with, but was not dependent on social and political upheavals and revolutions. Attitudes and opportunities would change, but the genius mentalities of those listed here were attuned to many other ingredients that found their way into their scores. Each composer probably had little patience with any particular prevailing war or political situation.

1750 – 1800 MOZART

The most significant happenstance during this period, and some would say for all periods, was the appearance of Wolfgang Amadeus Mozart (1757 – 91). Whatever happened in the seven or more years before his birth, and in his infancy served as a preparation for his appearance. Though his life was short, by the time he finished his last works in 1791, he had set in motion an empathetic reaction that continues to this day. His final years were negatively influenced by the calamity of the French Revolution, and the resultant fear felt by the Aristocracy. It was a fear that affected Mozart's ability to make money.

Mozart combined 1.) what he had heard and absorbed as a child on tour, 2.) as a roving juvenile and 3.) as a student in Italy, with his unique innateness to fuse all into an Art so superior as to make all his contemporaries seem dim in comparison. He excelled at form, instrumentation, chorus, or any medium he chose. Moreover, his music, when it is not just sounding pleasingly excellent, is streaked with emotional tinges that ensnare the ardent, faithful listener. If life involves a wide range of emotions, Mozart's music portrays as many as would be possible in that particular medium. His chief Instrumental media were Piano, Chamber Music, Concerto (especially those for Piano), Symphony, and Opera. He reigns as the chief Classist of all time. His forms were Ternary, Variations, Rondo, the dual theme Single--Movement Sonata, and the three or four movement assemblage. The emotional element mentioned above, sets his Instrumental Music apart from that of his chief contemporary, Haydn.

The many well--composed works of Franz Joseph Haydn (1732 – 1808) are an interesting backdrop to the supreme achievements of Mozart. Certainly Haydn was a giant presence in Europe throughout his own life. One can easily assume that Mozart, upon hearing the scores of Haydn, and choosing to emulate the forms established by the older composer, was impelled to even greater creativity. Mozart's other chief contemporaries were J. Sebastian's sons Emanuel and Christian, and Christoph Gluck. Beethoven would rise to prominence only after Mozart's death.

1800 – 1825 BEETHOVEN and NAPOLEON

Though this book attempts to ignore societal/political events in the lives of composers, it is not possible with Beethoven. Napoleon simply cannot be ignored or ruled out.

Even though he was in Vienna beginning in the early 1790s, Ludwig Van Beethoven's presence in the world of music was not fully felt until 1800, the year his Symphony No. 1 was premiered. In the late 1790s he had created piano sonatas and chamber works that had only modest effect on his reputation. He, and all Viennese, were nervously watching as French Society tore itself apart in the on--going class warfare. And after 1800 he witnessed the continent--wide chaotic "liberation" that Napoleon brought about for the next 15 years. With Napoleon as a contemporary, is it any wonder then that Beethoven would hold revolutionary notions about himself, and as to what music scores should depict or demonstrate? Relatively speaking, his scores would be revolutionary. Some qualities that can be named are 1.) expressing his own uniqueness, 2.) an occasional calculated excess in, tempos, instrumental use, and dynamics, and 3.) occasional juxtaposition of extreme tune and harmonic opposites. Beethoven described these effects as "dramatic." He also extended and varied the forms used by Mozart.

So, just as Napoleon's very existence dominated this quarter--century, so too, Beethoven's physical being dominated the concurrent music world. His 9 symphonies, 32 Piano Sonatas and 17 String Quartets, rightly or wrongly, would be a standard whereby all other coming music would often be judged.

SCHUBERT

Franz Schubert's entire Viennese short life (1792--1828) was lived in the shadow of Beethoven. It would have been hard for any musician in Vienna in this period to be unaware of Beethoven's Instrumental and Symphonic standing. So, Schubert strove for qualities in his own music that subtly stand apart from Beethoven's.

Thus Schubert's 20 or so Piano Sonatas, his 9 or 10 symphonies, as well as various chamber works do stand apart from Beethoven's in their consistent presentation of gentle song--like elements. Schubert, being a singer/pianist, also created some 700 Art Songs, a body of work that has held operatic and concert room singers and their audiences enthralled since their first piecemeal publication.

1825 – 1850 PIANO IS KING

After the Napoleonic turmoil and by 1820 European culture was finally regaining its composure. But with so many more "free" individuals, tastes of the ordinary man became all the more obvious and prevalent. Typical of this period were notions of fantasy, dream--like stories and legends. There was a surge in operas, especially in Paris, and in them fantasy subject matter would be used extensively. That element would also appear in Instrumental Music to the extent it could be suggested and depicted. But with or without a fantasy element, it may well be that what was written for piano during this period stands out as the most significant contribution to music.

The piano had been in existence since the latter half of the 1700s. By the early 1790s Mozart had created around 20 Sonatas as well as variations and other works. By the early 1800s Beethoven was leading the way in piano creations, and that continued almost up until his death. But in the 1820s Paris was a hotbed of piano instruction, and emerging artists. Newly formed companies were selling ever--improving pianos, and business was brisk. Budding piano composers and performers found their way to Paris from all over Europe. Against this backdrop a few significant composers were about to make their presence known, and they would feel the continuing shadow of Beethoven. A few would distinguish themselves as first--rate keyboard composers, and on occasion would they venture into Orchestral music.

Most famous at the time was the cosmopolitan and peripatetic Felix Mendelssohn. (1809 – 47) In addition to composing he branched into performance, conducting, administration, as well as choral, instrumental and symphonic music. His piano music is well--written, if occasionally overly sentimental. His five symphonies reveal a tuneful, dissonant--free music with little sense of drama as it is defined here. Instrumentalists then and now enjoy his idiomatic writing.

Robert Schumann (1810 – 56) started off creating a catalog of almost exclusively piano music (Twenty some opus numbers). Later in his life his four Symphonies reveal him to possibly be the most successful immediate successor to Beethoven in that medium.

The most impressive presence during this 25 year period is that of Frederic Chopin. (1810 – 1849) His main focus was piano music. It is not enough to say that he created a body of piano works that continue to be performed. In reality his legacy singles him out as perhaps piano's greatest composer, and more. His abstract pitch use (his pitch and rhythmic designs independent of the piano medium), his sense of drama, melodic skill and harmonic inventiveness make him a towering 1800s composer. Like Bach, his genius is revealed when studying the ideation in certain of his scores as if it were intended for any other medium. Most impressive are the *Preludes, Etudes, Ballades, Impromptus, Scherzos, Sonatas*, and the final *Polonaises*. (More are listed in Layer II.) Many 1800s composers who followed owe him a debt. Echoes of his music abound.

1850 – 1900 BRAHMS

It may be that Johannes Brahms (l833 – 97) is the most famous and successful reactionary composer of all time. His life mission seems to have been to return composition to the abstract movement of pitches on staves. He also seems to have had little patience with extra--musical ingredients in music such as plots, programs, depiction, etc. Music, he must have felt, had its own language and means towards artistic expression, and it dealt with the juxtaposition of beautiful and contrasting musical ideas. He was reverting to the former Beethoven way of constructing scores: thinking musically, and not entangling extra thoughts of plots and verbal meanings. The four Brahms symphonies more than attest to his supremacy as a composer. So, in retrospect, Brahms certainly is the dominating figure in the above 50--year cycle. And because of his stance, he was controversial in his time, a time when many were sure that opera and forms of it were the transcendent medium.

During Brahms' ascendancy his chief rival for fame was Richard Wagner (1813--83). But Wagner, and any other composers of opera during Brahms' lifetime were in a field, as was said earlier, not wholly musical. Opera was, and remains a separate entity from Abstract Music, and it is only loosely related to Music's historic ongoing progress. When it comes to Wagner's operas, the separate, and one might say, non--musical status becomes all the more obvious. As far as Music is concerned, Opera is in a special world of consideration, and deserves its own historic account. One can live a life experiencing music to its fullest without ever seeing or hearing an opera.

An outstanding contemporary of Brahms was Peter Tchaikowsky (1840–93), a master melodist and orchestrator. He is easily the most successful composer of all time in numbers of performances. His six or more symphonies and three ballets, have managed to stay in the collective minds of listeners since their first appearance during this 50--year period. Other important contemporaries of Brahms were Cesar Franck and Gabriel Faure.

Two more outstanding composers during the last years of the Brahms supremacy were the young Richard Strauss (l864 – 1949) and Gustav Mahler (1860 – 1911). Strauss created a number of depiction orchestral pieces that continue to excite audiences because of their sheer brilliance of orchestral sound. Mahler, on the other hand, embarked on a series of Symphonies that explore various dark and foreboding moods and states of mind. These Mahler works might well reflect the late l800s public psyche.

1900 – 1930 DEBUSSY and RAVEL

By 1900 change was in the air involving many aspects of European life. This was to be a new modern era. By then some composers were having trouble creating scores that were truly original. Had the "Tonality" way of composing simply exhausted itself? There would always be composers who were content to recycle old sounds, and sometimes the results were, and remain, admirable. To be fair to that approach, such composers often elected to "leaven" their scores with only a moderate use of truly new touches. Audiences were mostly on their side, for audiences wanted music to be a friendly comfort in the face of so many changes taking place in their world. Into this cultural situation enter Debussy and Ravel.

Even before 1900 Claude Debussy (l862 – 1918) was changing his approach to composition. For him, each new score would be conceived and built from the initial concept on up. Debussy, in fact, may be one of the most original composers of all time, considering the musical equalibrium with which he was surrounded. His harmony was truly revolutionary, while at the same time being attractive to a broad swath of the music public. Even though he always led with his melody, the very formal process in each of his mature scores seems invented and contrary to the formal processes then prevalent. And well they were. He finally achieved lasting recognition with his one finished opera, *Pelleas and Melisande*, 1902. Though his life ended in 1918, his effect endured into the l920s. Debussy had cast a large shadow.

A nearly exact contemporary also shares the spotlight in this period: Maurice Ravel (1875 – 1937). At the time (and beyond) many uninformed believed that the two were writing the same kind of music. A way of highlighting the difference between the two is the time--honored concept of chordal resolution. In the bulk of his scores, Debussy used his sometimes "Ravel--sounding" chords in a disjunct manner, rarely with traditional--sounding resolutions. This process could be called chordal succession. On the other hand Ravel used his sometimes "Debussy--sounding" chords always with a sense of near--traditional–sounding resolutions (but never V--I). Ravel was also careful to craft his melodies in traditional forms. Though Ravel continued composing for twelve or so years beyond Debussy's death, the dual identification continued. So long as Ravel remained alive, people felt the Debussy presence lingered. Outstanding works are Debussy's orchestral *Nocturnes*, and Ravel's *Daphnis et Chloe*.

Another composer who appeared during this period was the young Igor Stravinsky (1882--1971) whose pre--WWI ballets won instant recognition, popularity, and in one case (*The Rite of Spring*) notoriety. The lack of a Russian copyright agreement with the West enabled orchestras world--wide to play these exciting Russian scores, and well they did, scot--free, thus preventing Stravinsky from any financial benefit.

SIMULTANEOUS WITH DEBUSSY AND RAVEL (1900--30)

Try as it could, the music world, and indeed that of Composition could not be immune to the appalling cultural destruction, and even identity loss, brought on by WWI. How does a delicate, rarified Art like Concert/Recital Music survive, when all of political Europe seems bent upon blowing itself up? Still, there were some, if not many artistic endeavors that were in progress in 1914 that struggled through the war and were resumed in 1919.

Though there was much reformist thinking in this 30 year period, one particular type bears close attention. As the century began, Arnold Schoenberg (1874--1951) had been creating scores that seemed to plumb the depths of man's disturbed emotions. (Simultaneously Sigmund Freud was doing the same thing.) By 1914 Schoenberg and his followers were trying create a seemingly aphoristic music that was totally new in avoiding any hint of the old sounds of "Tonality." (Was this Atonality?) This music would certainly have an inner unifying structure, but it would also be nearly devoid of the "inefficiency" of pitch or "idea" repetition. Short--term note units, stated once, assiduously avoided the old tonality patterns. This was indeed a most radical departure from the time--honored methods of composing. There was even the suggestion of a new way of listening to the new music: study--listening. One studied the sounds one was hearing. Total originality was sought and achieved. Schoenberg and his followers claimed success, without ever addressing the need for audiences for such music. Maybe good--faith audiences were not, and never would be able to "study" and connect cerebrally--created pitch units. Much later, after 1920, while Europe was struggling to get back on its feet, Schoenberg developed a system whereby all 12 keyboard pitches would be in a chosen repetitive order and would rotate somewhat equally while simultaneously being a linear unifier during a composition's progress. The few adherents to this "system" retained and coveted it for a number of years.

Meanwhile, no matter what important compositional activities were taking place in the mainstream, there were always silly rumors that Schoenberg and his coterie were destroying all previous methods of composition. In reality they were aiming at an audience far into the future that would understand their Art.

1930 – 1950 BARTOK/STRAVINSKY/HINDEMITH

By 1930 Radio and phonograph recordings had become important factors in Composer Ascendency. In time these first vestiges of mass media would propel various genres of popular music that easily appealed to the masses. Symphonic/Chamber/Recital music thus became "High Art" that was understood and patronized by an unknown size of audience, certainly smaller than that of the masses. For a few decades this "High Art" could occasionally be heard on Radio, and after 1945 on Television as well. Economic hard times, and war were characteristic of this two--decade period. First there was a world--wide Depression immediately followed by WWII. All three of the above composers eventually took refuge in the United States. Bela Bartok (1885--1945) was famous earlier for his piano music and String Quartets. Until 1943, and for unknown reasons, he had written little for full orchestra. But the 1943 Boston Symphony Orchestra commissioning of his *Concerto for Orchestra* forever changed his image with the orchestral public.

Igor Stravinsky (1882--1971) had become known world--wide because of his three famous ballets, created just before WWI (*The Firebird*, *Petrushka* and *The Rite of Spring*). During that four--year war he continued creating scores while taking sanctuary in Switzerland. In the postwar '20s he was a famous persona in Paris who needed to earn money. He then adapted to the situation and secured lucrative commissions based on the fame of his name. In 1939 and 1945 he created two admirable symphonies that further enhanced his already legendary accomplishments. He would always be creating music for new ballets, Agon from the 1950s being the most famous. Also after 1950 he would redefine himself, producing a string of cerebral works that require study--listening. His name would symbolize prestige during and after his lifetime.

Paul Hindemith (1895--1963) is easily the most prolific of the three mentioned here. In his 1937 book, *The Craft of Composition*, he espoused Neo--tonality, in that at any given successions of measures, all twelve tones can be utilized, but some tones must be favored at the expense of others. Hindemith's approach to overtones in some respects matched Rameau's. Perfect 5ths were acoustical and therefore should be heard in melodies and harmony to verify important notes. He advocated and practiced using a mild form of dissonance, and that endeared him with a larger audience than would have been the case otherwise. He, too, needed money, so in the 1940s he took a professorial position at Yale University, and continued turning out one orchestral commission after another. Because of his prolific speed, there are times when the orchestral commissions sound insufficiently different from one another. However, there are occasional instances of profound beauty, such as the commission for the Dallas Symphony, the *Symphonia Serena*.

As one might expect, when WWII began in September 1939, European Culture was again forced into survival mode, but this time the "duck and take cover" was far more serious. Radio broadcasts became all the more important in the free world, even when it came to Symphonic/Chamber/Recital music. After five or so years the carnage ceased, and once again European culture emerged with an identity crisis. In late 1945 a number of European composers would gather in Darmstadt, Germany to try to piece together some semblance of identity and direction. And even then, conclusions and tendencies reached would be radical and only temporary.

1950 – 1970 ELLIOT CARTER and ROBERTO GERHARD

By the 1950s some patterns in composition began to emerge. There would always be a mainstream of works that were sensible and somewhat easy to understand for audiences. But the 1950s also signaled the beginning of an ultra--modernist movement. Beginning at this time and on into the 1960s the game for some aspiring composers was to "out modernize" one another. Certainly brilliant minds were producing stunning ground--breaking scores, aided by limited--sale commercial recordings. But aside from a small but ardent following, how did a larger potential audience fit into this situation?

Elliot Carter (1908 – 2012) at first singled himself out for attention immediately following WWII with his remarkable Piano Sonata. That work seems almost improvisational in its avoidance of any semblance of a regular beat. Around the same time he produced a Cello Sonata that may have been the first to feature tempo modulation (changes of tempo are smoothed over so as to be almost imperceptible). Beginning in the 1950s his first String Quartet brought even more attention. Then throughout the 1950s he began to produce a string of orchestral works that, while not using serial techniques, challenged the listener with full--fledged dissonance, tightly controlled melodic lines, rhythmic flow and interaction. As his career continued, Carter would explore total picture complexity as a form of musical expressiveness. By 1970 he was about to test the limits of density, as demonstrated in his 3rd String Quartet. In the final decades of his enormously long career, he would eventually step back into less complexity in a number of chamber works. If any composer's work could be described as stimulatingly cerebral, resulting in more respect than love, Carter's would be paramount. His *Variations for Orchestra* warrants multiple hearings.

In 1950 Roberto Gerhard (1896 – 1970) was 54 years old. Born in Spain, he immigrated to England during the Franco purge. Up until 1950 he had attracted little attention from the music world at large even though he was compositionally active. As the 1950s began he was about to create his career-- changing work, his First Symphony. Its London premiere had all the London critics ecstatic. Even today recordings of this work defy description. It combines dissonant lines and agreeable harmony, perceptible form, and rhythmic/motivic repetitive procedures that insure a satisfying information delivery. There is also an emotional essence that captures the willing listener. If anything, and without intending, Gerhard is saying to the composition world, "This is how it can and should be done." Gerhard's later 2nd Symphony was perhaps his most experimental. It was supposedly created using some sort of system. It has a first movement that is simultaneously incomprehensible and engrossing. The final two movements are much shorter, are clearly understood and are almost hypnotic.

By the mid '50s the orchestral commissions for Gerhard were coming in steadily, perhaps because of his skill at making the modern symphony orchestra sound engagingly modern and compelling, and he was becoming more widely known. His 3rd Symphony utilized electrosonics, and by his own admission, was programmatic in that spots were descriptive of experiences while jetting over the Atlantic. His 4th Symphony (a portrait of New York

City) is another masterpiece of information delivery involving emotional and rhythmically kinetic content. Repeated playing of recordings prove its force and effect. There is also an inimitable *Concerto for Orchestra*. What Carter's music lacks in emotive sensuousness, Gerhard's provides in abundance.

THE REST OF THE PICTURE (1950--70)

In the decades before 1950 Henry Cowell and John Cage had set the stage for followers who would also question what a musical experience should be. Noises, discords and happenstance, they felt, were potential music, too. A number of like--minded up--coming composers would often blend extra-- musical features in their creations in imaginative ways. For a while small and excited audiences would welcome the newness of it all. Some of the high profile figures in this ultra--modernist effort were Karlheinz Stockhausen, Pierre Boulez, Luciano Berio, Ianis Xenokis, Heinze Werner Henze, and, after decades of seeking attention, Edgar Varese.

Electronic Music had its beginnings a little after the end of WWII. French individuals had their Musique Concrete (the processing of acoustical sounds on magnetic tape), and some German individuals had their manipulation of purely electronic generated sounds. In both cases the sounds (electrosonics) were strikingly new to all listeners. In time a few composers in America and more in Europe were creating their own sound poems that explored sounds that had never before been heard. However, all such works would unfortunately be forever locked in their magnetic tape medium. Gone was the timeless process of live human performers bringing music back to life in new regenerative versions. Some Tape works did combine live instruments with electrosonics, thus partially correcting the situation. Even so, for an indeterminate number of coming decades new and expressive sonic creations would excite a limited audience.

As an annual event, the annual Pulitzer Prize in Music did its best to call attention to American composers. Winning resulted in some degree of fame as well as some performances and recording purchases. In addition to the Americans mentioned above (Cowell and Cage), prize winners were William Schuman, Howard Hanson, Charles Ives, Walter Piston, Virgil Thompson, Ross Lee Finney, Leslie Bassett and (through their operas) Virgil Thompson and Gian Carlo Menotti. There were of course others, each distinguishing themselves with outstanding scores. But overall, this is just the surface of a situation where many composers were creating many outstanding scores.

AFTER 1970

Much will challenge a future writer in organizing the world of High--Art Composition after this year. A number of approaches and their constituencies played a part.

First and foremost there is "the elephant in the room:" Popular music. A specialized faction of it would be Jazz, an inherently improvised medium. Its exponents, performers and audiences, never that large, would support it through thick and thin, decade after decade. Its rarified rhythms and approaches made it an insulated faction of Popular music, almost immune to quick fashion changes. It began after WW I, and continued throughout the century.

However, the culture of Popular music had a presence that would grow and grow, capturing huge swaths of the population, worldwide. Even the quality of the product itself would be lowered so as to appeal to the widest possible denominator of listener. In its success fortunes would be made, careers would rise and fall, and musical examples would come and go as part of an intended quick profit and obsolescence. Short--term memory among the customers was counted upon. In time its patronage would become a zealously guarded manner of life, completely cut off from music thought to be too complex to hear or patronize. Popular music became increasingly ubiquitous, and High--Art Music became increasingly marginalized, especially the Modernistic kind.

Certain individualistic composers would, as they always had, create scores that blended the newest techniques with elements of the past. Maybe, they reasoned, the sought--after larger audience would more easily understand and patronize something that was related closer to the long line of Music History. Others would incorporate elements of popular music in an almost futile effort to reach a wider following.

Against this backdrop some radical patterns that had begun before 1970 would continue that in time would fizzle out. For instance, 12--Tone Serialists would continue their creations for their few followers, in the face of general apathy at large. Electronic Composition of the analog type would in time fizzle. The unique sounds being manipulated were no longer new, and complications of performance set--ups for live audiences were becoming too inconvenient. Analog Electronic Music would also be further killed by the up--coming Digital Music mirage. (Mirage because it went nowhere.) The small audiences for all manner of electronically or digitally created music would survive through recordings heard in living rooms, and in annual highly specialized festivals and contests.

A return to intuitive/Romantic score creation began in the 1970s, spurred on by attention to the (then) newly recorded film scores of Erick Wolfgang Korngold (1897 – 1957). Korngold had created his Romantic--style, attractive scores between 1936 and 1947, and the newer 1970s recordings set off a craze for more of such music. Even recordings that featured background music for scenes by other film composers were a viable product for sale. This led to large audiences who wanted their High--Art Music to be less cerebral and more humane.

The result was/is a Neo--Romantic period, sometimes referred to as a Post–Modern period. As a result of this turn of events, one famous high--profile serialist composer reverted to creating scores almost in the manner of Bartok. The annual Pulitzer Prizes would continue, but would lean more in the direction of scores that were more recognizably humane. A list of the prize--winning scores after 1971 will confirm that.

Another compositional trend would be that of Minimalism. Musical ideas within a work would be repeated excessively with only slight changes. Sometimes the emphasis would be on an incessant beat (Phase--minimalism?). Maybe the composer was counting upon the listener's brain being lulled into submission. Such music would attract much larger audiences comprised of individuals who would not have to pay much attention, but rather just surrender to obvious sound patterns being repeated ad--infinitum.

There were John Cage imitators who expanded music to mean all manner of life, sounds and incongruity. There would be music intended as atmosphere, and not meant to be attended to with any degree of rationality. There were several manifestations of Extentialism: Among them was Music that should be heard only once; and "Music that doesn't have to go anywhere," but merely exists to be heard without any expectations of interior score growth. There would be composers who did not trust their creative minds to come up with originality, and who would therefore rely on various types of external non--musical determinants to create complete scores. There were also those who used technology or other means to arrive at raw material which would then be intuitively woven into scores. There would be attempts to create all manner of new music initiatives that were obviously distinctly separate from the past.

This is just an incomplete account of High--Art Music after 1970, and it will be up to a future writer to determine a sensible overview.

LAYER II

ANCIENT TIMES

(You are encouraged to review all categories in Layer I.)

In the time of the Ancient Greeks, and in fact in all civilizations then existing, music was regarded as having magical curing powers. The writings of Homer and the Bible attest to it. Ancient Greeks who identified with Apollo favored the Lyre, and those who identified Dionysus favored the Aulos (a double reed wind instrument). A large form of the Lyre was called the Kithara. These had 5 to 11 strings. The Greeks had contests and festivals involving these, and other various instruments.

Music was monophonic (just a melody and text) with the above mentioned instruments in support. Somehow dance was even involved. Ethos involved the moral qualities inherent in the music, and the Greeks felt that human behavior was linked to the particular Ethos in the music. Since the Greeks were concerned with developing well--balanced men who were not too sensitive (precious), nor crude in manner, the right Ethos in music supposedly helped to bring about a balance.

Tuning of instruments was reliable, having the benefit of Pythagoras' experiments and writings early in the Greek Ancient Period. The later Greeks developed a scale system based on the small four-- contiguous note unit called the Tetrachord. Their scales would always be limited by the ranges of the male voice. What we would call an eight--note scale, for them involved two stacked tetrachords. A tetrachord had a constant frame of a perfect 4th. The two notes within the frame, however, were adjustable. When one considers the stacking of Tetrachords and the movable notes, one can easily imagine scalar effects that ranged from rarefied/exotic, all the way to our modern diatonic (and other) scales.

Unlike modern thinking though, the Greeks began with a point--of--reference pitch, to which added pitches continued downward. When confronted with what the Greeks wrote about their scales, and their attached labels, later Christian writers were motivated to emulate them. (Even if the later thinkers got the direction wrong in successive pitches.) If any factor was/is frustrating to modern scholars and students, it was the Ancient Greek tendency to label every scale degree, or any other unit, with unique multi--syllabic names. (Imagine trying to multiply numbers using only the long-- hand labels of each number!) The Greeks were concerned with the highest and lowest notes possible from the male voices, and so for theoretical thinking, they conceived of the Greater Perfect System, something akin to our grand staff.

THE EARLIEST CHRISTIAN ERA

At first the Christians avoided music because of its association with Pagan life. In time, and somewhat influenced by Jewish ritual music, the Western Christians created their own own monophonic religious songs for use in the Mass. After 313 Byzantium/Constantinople Christians would in time be heavily influenced by Greek Culture. And, being closer to Asia Minor they seemed to have created music for their religious ceremony that was even more obviously influenced by Jewish ritual. Here, too, the music was monophonic. In time all of their melodies were organized into a system of eight types (four pairs) called *echoi*. We will see a parallel organization in the Western Church. Each of the eight categories was unified by similar melodic material, rather than any particular scale. Heard today, one is struck by the amount of elaboration in the Eastern melodies.

600 ---- 800

The authorities in Rome certainly had their hands full, dealing with enclaves all around the Western Mediterranean. Both Eastern and Western Christianity had the enormous task of systematizing diverse musical practices from far--flung geographic locations. In the West the Pope would eventually initiate a standardization, while still maintaining a respect for the practices of diverse enclaves. Gregory I (Pope from 590--604) is credited with the organization of what is now called Gregorian Chant. Later on, the Western Church, would organize all its sacred melodies (with texts) into eight categories (four pairs) according to scale type.

Organization became necessary, not so much for the ordinary Christian who would be exposed to frequently--heard chant melodies during Masses. There were only so many Masses, and the melodies to the most repeated parts of the Mass were frequently heard. But there were short chant melodies attached to specific calendar dates that would change from day to day, and they needed attention. More specifically, organization was all the more important in the monasteries, with their eight--times daily use of chant melodies. What was passed on to newcomers had to be uniform. Consistency was required. The results of the massive organization Gregorian Chant, can be heard piecemeal today. And as a body of work, it stands out as a highpoint in Music History. The Ambrosian Hymn tradition, differing from the Gregorian and practiced in the region of Milan, was allowed to continue.

800 – 1000

Maybe it was the formation of the Holy Roman Empire around 800, and maybe it was the crowning of French king Charlemagne as its first Emperor, with the promise of firm government and less turmoil that brought about the next advances. It is hard to say why, but important musical developments began at this time. (Described in Layer I) Though improvements came about in scattered geographical locations, they did take place.

EIGHT CATEGORIES – FOUR PAIRS

In the process of organization, the Church would never be happy using the old Greek labels for their modes/scales, and in time they would eliminate them. But for the time being, and based on misreading what the Ancient Greeks meant, they settled on four over--all types: Dorian, starting on D (and ascending); Phrygian, starting on E; Lydian, starting on F; and Mixolydian, starting on G. Because those scales favored the soprano and tenor ranges, it was necessary to accommodate the lower range alto and baritone voices, so plagal forms were added: Dorian Plagal, Phrygian, Plagal, Lydian Plagal and Mixolydian plagal. Now, imagine the difficulty of sorting all melodies into these eight categories without benefit of a written notation.

Having organized chant melodies, or merely having tried to do so, the musicians concentrated on perceived formulas the melodies exhibited while fitting into each melody's perceived mode. They noticed and codified chant final notes, and the frequented reciting tones. They noticed that B was a note to be largely avoided because of its devilish tendency to create a tritone interval with F. It may have been at this time that B flats began being improvised to avoid the tritone. When the organizers were finished, they knew they had fulfilled the eight--mode challenge, even though some melodies were a careless fit, with convenient cadences tacked on. Surprisingly, as was said earlier, the organizers did all this without a written notation.

In early the 900s Odo of Cluny, or one of his students limited the seven notes (on our imaginary keyboard) to just one label each: A through G. This may have been the first time scale degrees were implied to be one through seven. Odo's innovation held.

During these two centuries instruction of young singers had necessarily proliferated. Just before year 1000 Guido of Arezzo had created a syllable system that was gleaned from the *Hymn to Saint John*. In that hymn successive phrases begin on notes that form a rising six--note hexachord/scale (ut – re – me – fa – sol – la). This is also just a hair's width away from putting rising numbers on each scale degree. Guido used these scalar labels to teach young singers. In time he made some extensions of the principle, and in so--doing revolutionized the teaching process. One of the extensions was the creating another "grand staff" of sorts. Imagine a low g in the baritone range, going up to a high e in the soprano range, made up of overlapping hexachords from low to high. All extant musical activity would take place in that master range.

Another significant advance, though only a glimmer, was the first appearance of harmony brought about through singing in parallel perfect intervals. Admittedly these were faltering steps towards voice independence and harmony, but the steps were taken. The Enchiriadis Manuscripts (from around 900), in a crude but decipherable notation, indicate multiple voices moving in parallel motion. It is impossible to say how long this musical practice had been in effect before the writing of these manuscripts, but one wonders.

1000 – 1200

Secular and religious songs began appearing in manuscripts. A prominent type was the Galliard (or student) Songs. Some of these are in the (by--then) advancing notation on a staff. Another type in the new notation was Procession songs called Conductus/Conducti. Yet another instance in the evolving notation is France's ancient epic poem, *The Song of Roland*.

Travelling Jongleurs, who were itinerant and illiterate entertainers, made it possible for isolated communities to hear political rumors, and changing fashions in secular song. Higher up on the social scale, and fulfilling the same function as the Jongleurs, were the Minstrels who stayed in castles or towns. All such worldly, secular, life--affirming activity was most evident in a bastion of wealth, Occitania, consisting of conjoined castle fiefdoms in Southern France near Provence. Here was a largely free--thinking society with its own form of the French language, tolerant of non--Christians and even novel religious ideas. A number of its aristocrats were Troubadours (finders) who created poems and monophonic songs, many of which are preserved in staff--notation. This island of liberality was marked for complete destruction by the greedy Capetian French Throne, and the impossibly narrow thinking of the Papacy. All sin would thus be supposedly obliterated and Occitania's wealth assumed by the victors. So, a little after 1200 Occitania and most of its culture, and especially free--thinking was annihilated.

1200s THE NOTRE DAME SCHOOL and THE SIX RHYTHMIC MODES

In this instance modes means method or procedure. This rhythmic method had probably been in effect in Paris since the late 1100s, and there is some scant evidence that it may have even been in effect in one or more religious communities/monasteries in outer provinces. With a continuum of compound beats (Picture half of a 6/8 measure with its three beat--partials.) the singer would use one of the modes to execute one or more continuous phrases. For instance, it might be as an on--going long--short, long--short delivery. That was Mode I. Mode 2 was on--going short--long, Mode 3 would be two full beats, and so--forth, utilizing only the most basic of rhythms in our modern 6/8 meter. The sacred chant melody would move at the rate of beats. Other separate voices were now somewhat independent, and would simultaneously move slightly faster in and out of beats that featured acceptable harmony. (Only perfect 5ths or octaves on the beat.) It was religious music that brought this about, and it was a significant advance in rhythm and harmony.

In the 1200s Parisian scheme of things there were also three types of basic textures involving two or three simultaneous voices. There are surviving manuscripts that indicate them. The first texture was homorhythm, or at least the effect of near homorhythm. (To use a 20th century concept: block chords, but the harmony was restricted to that explained above.) This is the texture found in conductus/conducti. The second texture had the most extreme difference in voice speeds. While most of the choir and the organ accompaniment played a slow--moving chant line, a single soloist would devise all manner of quick notes. One clear modern name for this is "Pound--Note" texture. The third texture is frequently called the Discant Clausula, and is perhaps the most influential in the development of polyphony/ harmony. While voices and organ moved through a chant melisma at moderate speed, one or two rhythmically independent added voices would move slightly faster through acceptable harmonies, thus this would be a forerunner of two-- and three--voice counterpoint. Singers of the faster voices would add somewhat appropriate texts of their own, sometimes in early French, and the result would be called a Motet. (*Mot* is French for word.)

The century saw the flourishing of monophonic religious songs, usually involving prayers to the Virgin. These were an outgrowth of the Troubadour/Trouvere songs. Over in Germany Aristocratic love--song composers were actively incorporating AAB forms into their creations. The century saw songs and dances known as *Estampie*. That such secular music would survive in manuscript form is a testament that man was moving forward culturally, unencumbered by religious fear. Frequent instruments (apparently) were bowed fiddle-- types and other stretched string instruments for strumming, barrel organ prototypes, harps, bagpipes, drums and organs in three sizes: large, portable, and table--top.

In 1272 John Garland died. We are indebted to him for his explanations of the Six Rhythmic Modes. In 1288 Adam De la Halle died, and he is considered the last and greatest of the Trouveres. And, above all, there is the cherished work of Franco of Cologne, also dying at this time, who established that a certain note symbol lasted twice as long as another that looked different. That was new.

1300s

This century saw many troubles. The economy began wavering, the Black Death, exactly at mid-- century, reduced much of the population. The Plague and money problems easily led to urban and peasant discontent, and the Aristocracy began losing its grip, thus leading in some instances towards separate independent political status for some commoners. Troubles in the Church (1305 – 1378) led to the authority of the Papacy being questioned. Hence, if there could be several simultaneous popes, there could also be room for free thinking or heretical initiatives. Man's reasoning could now be seen as differing from God's. The Plantagenet Wars against the Capetian French kings began in 1338 and continued half--way into the next century. But this was also a century of positive change and increasing multiformity. There was growth in vernacular literature, and there were exciting innovations in painting, and in Humanism (a way of seeing man's place in the scheme of things).

THE FOUR PROLATIONS

(Formally and inclusively put: Modus (mood),Tempus (time), Prolatio (Prolation). Modus and Tempus would refer to groupings of our measures.)

Much music was being written, especially using the new options 2/2 or 4/4. (We can label the meters thusly, but the then prevalent method of Four Prolations would label and notate them differently, using no bar lines.) Never had there been so much secular music created. The Prolations also made possible a variety of new rhythms. Harmonic 3rds and 6ths began appearing with more frequency, and some composers were hearing more harmonically. Humanism meant that music could appeal to man's feelings, and these new music techniques would help composers in that appeal.

As the century began, an Italian method of notation (seen in scores by Petrus de Cruce) was gaining ground. Though it was built on Franconian principles, it allowed a flexibility in dividing the beat into possible triplets, quadruplets, quintuplets, etc. In time the Italian notation method lost out to the French Four Prolations. It was also at this time in Italy that the word Madrigal first appeared as a label for short songs with refrains.

There seems to have been little English music of high merit during the 1300s. However, the English tendency to favor harmonic 3rds and 6ths, twin voice movement, and (what we would call) parallel 6/3 chords would eventually influence coming continental music. English musicians were ahead of their time in favoring music with little or no cerebral planning (Isometers, excessive reliance on the perfect intervals). Even earlier, around 1300, English Theorists officially recognized the 3rd as consonant, and so their music abounded in them. They also favored music that sounds to us like major tonality, as well as singly--proclaimed, easily understood texts.

Two outstanding composers at the time were Guillaume de Mauchaut in France, and the twenty years younger Francesco Landino/Landini in Italy. Whereas Mauchaut's music was (and remains) rife with subtlety, rhythmic display, hollow 5ths and 4ths, dissonant clashes and other intellectual content, it was the blind Landino/Landini who created a more triad--inclusive music that easily leads into the coming music of the next century. All music of the 1300s was slowly moving towards (what we would call) harmonic (triadic) organization, the appreciation of harmonic effects, more and more avoidance of dissonant clashes between voices, clearly heard texts, and more pieces in the Cantilena/Ballade style. However, throw--back Isorhythmic pieces would continue on into the next century.

1400 -- 1450

The Parisian (Notre Dame) music of the 1300s was known in England, and it is reflected in English music. A giant manuscript (found in Scotland) reflects music from this period. It has 24 English composers, and 148 pieces of music that are for use during Mass. The texture in all pieces is conservative with modified block--chords. (Conductus -- like) There are Gregorian melodies in every piece. There are also 6/3 chords in isolation and in stepwise parallel motion. (The 6/3 label is a modern appellation. The musicians at the time thought in terms of small intervals that were combined.)

John Dunstable emerges as the most important composer of the early 1400s. Serving his English monarch, his presence and activities on French soil during the Plantagenet wars clearly influenced continental musicians. Maybe he singularly induced the coming Musical Renaissance. His music is potent and solely triadic with no dissonance, producing an effect of "joy" and "pleasantness." There are 60 known works, only 12 of which are in (throw--back) Isorhythm.

The younger continental Guillaume Dufay (1400 – 74) would be the principle composer of the 1400s. He would be the inspiration for a coming trove of choral riches by succeeding Renaissance composers. It is therefore easy to imagine the effect on Dufay upon first hearing any Dunstable works. It would later be a matter of Dufay blending his mastery of four--part writing with the triadic continuum heard in Dunstable's work, but this time, and for expressive purposes, there would be a modest use of dissonance. Dufay would use Passing Tones and Suspensions to make the strong and weak metric positions all the more obvious. Inner and final cadences would sometimes give the sound of what, much later in Music History, would be called V--I cadences. Each individual voice would reflect Dufay's sense of elegantly balanced linear beauty. Dufay would produce Masses and Motets, frequently in four voices. Favorite Chant melodies of the day, along with secular melodies would somehow be woven into the choral fabric, and would give each work a title that reflected the source material. With Dufay's music, we have the beginning of the musical Renaissance. Here was the groundwork upon which succeeding composers could build.

Dufay's chief contemporary was an associate of the (then) powerful Burgundian court, Gilles Binchois, who was perhaps the greatest composer of Cantelina/Ballade works. By the time he died in 1460 he had created Songs, Masses and other sacred music, all in incipient monody (melody and accompaniment). The sung line was often a Gregorian melody with extra expressive decorous notes woven in. Both Dufay and Binchois created (throw--back) Isometric works, probably in keeping with contemporaneous expectations.

Another name for Masses based on borrowed melodies is Tenor Mass. Most frequently the borrowed melody would be referred to as the "Tenor," and that word somehow means a kept melody. It would be placed second from the bottom, where today's notion of the tenor voice range belongs. Another label that collectively refers to this type is Cantus Firmus

Mass. Whereas we would say the familiar style consists of Soprano – Alto -- Tenor and Bass, back then the reasoning was (all male) Superius, the highest voice freely created; high (alto) countertenor just above the borrowed melody; Tenor, the borrowed melody; and low (bass) countertenor. The "bass" voice was freely composed and more easily cooperated in controlling the triadic change. There were slight range differences when compared with modern SATB reasoning. And unlike more modern practice, there would be much crossing of voices. The most borrowed melody was "The Armed Man," a secular tune that gave rise to many Masses created between 1450 and the 1560s.

THE RENAISSANCE (in music) BEGINS 1450 -- 1500

A group of composers succeeded Dufay and were led by Josquin des Pres. (See Layer I) Josquin, along with his important contemporaries prevailed up to about 1520. They were Johannes Ockeghem, Jacob Obrecht, Antoine Busnois, Henricus Isaac and Pierre de la Rue. Each, in their own particular style, had built upon what Dufay had established. Each, including Josquin, added imitation to the four--part fabric. The imitation aspect was new. An idea heard in one voice would seemingly be mimicked in other voices. Such Imitation was lightly applied, usually at entrances of lines. Extreme imitation (Canon), where one line is sung in succession by all sections was respected but rarely used. Ockeghem, however, has the distinction of having created the perfect Canon Mass.

1500s – CHORAL MUSIC IN THE ASCENDENCY

The first half of the 1500s seemed to have no single outstanding composer. Josquin's last twenty years, ending in 1520, were that of a senior master whose earlier works, published in 1501, stood as an inspiring challenge to those who would follow. The following are composers of note whose work, though well crafted, did not stand out as a dominant force for musical advancement. All were active during the first half of the century : Nicholas Gombert, Jacob Clement, Ludwig Senfl and Adrian Willaert. It was in their motets that one finds compositionally progressive practices.

An important type of piece appeared in Italy in the early 1500s called the Frottola. It involved casual song in common tongue, and it was melody accompanied with block chords. This type of piece was important because it led to the development and flowering of the Madrigal, beginning in the 1530s. The Frottola, in terms of its texture was an outgrowth of Cantilena/Ballad style that had been continuing from earlier centuries. Whereas the singer in earlier centuries was accompanied by two supporting lines that often help form triads, the Frottola now had block chords, usually played on lute--family instruments. That the Frottolla grew into the Madrigal is significant. Not to be outdone, the French would create their equivalent version of the Frottola. Famous composer names there would be Claudin dc Sermisy, Clement Janequin, and Pierre Certon. Following suit in the Netherlands would be Gombert, Clemens non Papa and others.

During this flurry of casual songs with chordal accompaniment generally in Italy and France, the rather staid and proper Germans were concerned more with casual songs that were in a three--voice contrapuntal setting. The Spaniards early in the century, while giving some evidence of casual song settings, were far more interested in Sacred Polyphony. English composers, under the Tudor Monarchs, had their minds on other matters. Composers in that country throughout most of the century were careful to appear to be either Protestant, or Catholic, depending on which religion was then occupying the throne.

Instead of a mid--1500s all--important composer, the Madrigal stands out as a major achievement. Originally an Italian innovation; it would be imitated in other languages and countries. Linear imitation was of course a natural feature, along with experimental musical moves and sometimes animated effects. It utilized native Italian casual poetry of no striking literary merit, but showed it off to great effect. Poetic strophes and sections were blurred, refrains were avoided, and when possible the use of notes would depict the meaning of separate words and phrases.

By the mid--century Madrigals were in four equal voices, but in the second half of the century five voices became the norm. There were instances of even more voices. The use of five voices was also typical of Masses and other kinds of Choral Music of the time. The Madrigal was "sitting room" music in that well--born soloists were assigned each part. Difficult musical moves were made possible because of the expertise of the singers, and each singer competed to keep up with the rest. Instruments would routinely double each singer's part, and in some instances would even stand in for missing singers.

The impressive work of Palestrina marks a fitting close to the 1500s. Beside him would be Roland Lassus (1532--94) standing almost as significantly. Both abided by the reforms of the Council of Trent, and both composed in all the accepted choral forms common to the century. Scholars in later centuries would single out the music of Palestrina for its beauty through restraint. To know his work is to realize why there have been consistent efforts at emulation. As in all Renaissance choral music, triads are presented in seeming random succession, with no effort at returning familiar progressions. In the hands of Palestrina and Lassus, the results are singable, admirable and transcendent.

Also at the end of the 1500s, and following the defeat of the Spanish Armada, England experienced supreme dramatic achievements. (This was the time of Shakespeare.) There were also outstanding musical achievements, with a boon in English language madrigals. The English were apparently celebrating their newly found national strength and independence. Famous names are Morley, Weelkes, Willbye, and Byrd. Lutenists John Dowland and Thomas Campion also distinguished themselves. Coincidently in Italy Prince Carlo Gesualdo of Venosa was creating a book of Italian Madrigals that employed successions of remotely related triads. These were chromatic chord changes were taken to the extreme. It was a technique that would reappear in the 20th Century.

All through the 1500s there were glimmers of instrumental music, often in conjunction with dance, using such instruments as pre--violin string types, along with lute, wind and harpsichord types. Drums were also used to emphasize strong beats. Surviving Variation and Dance scores show that melodic instrumentalists were playing many notes per beat. Even with evidence of instrumental music activity, the choral period would not give up its ascendency until around l600. England was slightly behind the times in that its "Renaissance period" of choral riches continued for a decade or so beyond 1600.

LEADING UP TO 1600

Many of the developments in the early 1600s had already been started in the late 1500s. Some had even begun earlier in that century, but to little effect. The full impact of these developments, however, would be felt in the 1600s. For instance Lutheran Chorales began much earlier than 1600, but only became more obvious in the coming century. After 1600 it was clear the Chorale texture involved block chords, with the melody in the highest voice. The congregation was helped with support from the organ. It was also after 1600 that organists were performing Chorales in elaboration. Certain Protestant faiths accepted music only in its barest form. Psalters date from this time that show melodies, devoid of any accompaniment. Out of orders from the monarch, English Anglican church music began its existence after 1550. The composers were the same names associated earlier with Catholic music, and later with English Madrigals. The Anglican church formulated the so--called Service which vaguely resembled the Catholic Mass. Motets now became newly composed Anthems with English lyrics.

Losing much ground to the Protestant movement, the Catholic Church reacted by instituting far-- reaching changes to take effect after 1563. Only the changes dealing with music will be described here. There would be no Masses that referred to secular songs in their titles. The fact that a secular song could be woven into the Mass texture, be distorted and undetected was accepted. It was the title practice that was banned along with a warning and plea recommending that the religious text be more decipherable by those attending Mass. That could be tricky for the composers. The established method of counterpoint meant that not all sections of the choir were saying the same Latin words at the same time. For a while certain Bishops recommended a rejection of counterpoint altogether, in favor of block chordal writing. In time though, and with some persuasion and demonstrations, most of the bishops voted to retain counterpoint, but with occasional interspersions of block chordal (homorhythmic) writing.

The most prominent Catholic composer (mentioned earlier) who lived through the near--purge was Palestrina. In time he ended up demonstrating the highest artistic levels of artistry and appropriate piety. Eventually the Catholic Church preserved his nearly seven hundred works in expensively produced editions. Even his secular works were preserved. Also, as indicated earlier, the musical procedures Palestrina used were those largely demonstrated by Josquin in the late 1400s. Palestrina was not a stylistic trail--blazer, but the results of his work reach the heights of possible beauty. Important contemporaries of Palestrina were Luis de Victoria, and the earlier mentioned Rolland Lassus (Orlando di Lasso). Lassus easily challenges Palestrina as the greatest composer in the late 1500s. If anything prevents him from being so, it is the sheer variety, stylistic inconsistency, and the many group types for which he composed. His style is not easy to pin down. However, one can still appreciate his sometimes surprising harmonic changes, and the "warmer" effect he achieves.

INSTRUMENTAL MUSIC

In the late 1500s there was an established practice of playing instrumental versions of choral works, especially among organists. Eventually groups of instruments would do the same. At the time the label for such works was Canzona. As the 1600s got under way, the Canzona could be seen developing into later typical Baroque forms, such as the Fugue and the Church Sonata. By the late 1500s dance pairs under various titles had come about. They usually involved a slow piece, followed by a fast. With the Canzona spin--offs and the dance pairs, the l600s were seeing inherently instrumental music, a typical and innovative feature of the Baroque period.

Early in the 1600s organists were creating various pieces that merely emphasized finger technique. They went under various names: Fantasies, Preludes, Toccata, etc. When measured against works from the later Baroque period, the harmonic direction of these earliest pieces can be quite random, and hence ineffective to careful listeners. But the required finger technique can be impressive. The same observations and criticisms could be made of many of the English Virginal (harpsichord) pieces of this same time period.

The music heard in Saint Mark's Cathedral in Venice during the late 1500s was perhaps the most advanced in all of Europe. There was an atmosphere of inventiveness and innovation, all supported by the then existing City/State government. Choral music, instrumental ensembles and solo organ reflected a new spirit of ostentation that predicted practices common to the later 1600s. Venetian music was thus well ahead of its time. Most of this music was performed at the above--mentioned famous cathedral where there were two choir lofts facing one another at not too great a distance. That situation invited, and resulted in opposing musical groups responding to one another in block-- chordal writing. Because instruments were easily involved in one or both opposing groups, the coming art of orchestration was advanced one preliminary notch.

The 1600 -- 1650

Excluding the late English Madrigal decades, and the birth of Opera, this period is one of few musically historic achievements. Blame it on war. Two major countries that would have seen advances in music were having their own internal turmoil. The German states were enduring the Thirty Years War (Protestant states versus Catholic), and England a Puritan anti--Monarch civil war. For some composers Italy proved a relatively war--free haven. There are a few traceable continental composers (Monteverdi, Schutz) on whom one could focus, but other than for them, musical progress in retrospect, seems very slow. There were a few high--profile opera events, at this time still a brand new medium, but little else in this fifty--year period. Meanwhile Instrumental Music was sheltered and busy making headway.

1650 – 1700

There would be phenomenal musical growth in these fifty years, a veritable proliferation of developments. (Maybe the reign of Louis 14, during this same time frame, helped amid other conditions to create a secure stability.) One achievement was the accelerated growth in Instrumental Music. And, like all major achievements, some individuals and their activities were well ahead of the particular starting year 1650.

FURTHER ADVANCES IN INSTRUMENTAL MUSIC

Without texts, music could potentially stymie listeners. Abstract music had to have new ways for comprehension. There were problems to solve. Choral composition meant that even the most beautiful of pieces moved in a relatively staid rhythmic stodginess. Certain animated madrigals would suggest ways that instrumental music might likewise be more rhythmic and animated. Also, coherent harmonic progressions had to be developed. Random triadic changes, so common in previous choral music, would not do. Figured bass, now more increasingly prominent, made that need more obvious in that musicians were listening for a naturalness in the chord changes. And there were all those speedy notes made possible on violins and keyboards that cried out for a controlling factor in handling desired fast note redundancy. What was needed was an anchor of recognizable harmonic-- progressions, forms and formulas that would recur from work to work, and those would indeed come about.

The practices of composers in the Italian states would be observed and copied by musicians from other countries. But just what were the Italians doing? Since 1637 they showed that opera could be staged in public theaters for the entertainment of a wider swath of the population. Also, operas were using so--called Sinfonias as introductions and filler in lulls.

This would be imitated in the north. In their operas the Italian composers seemed to be at times entrancing learned and upper class audiences with what could be described as a repetitive casual chattering of instruments. The newly adopted violin would excel at this with facile ease. Composers were also infusing their operas with intensely emotional arias that could be attempted in solely instrumental writing. Operas were showing that certain other moods or emotional states could also be simulated. And, above all, operas thrived on sudden radical (dramatic) change. This, too, could be emulated in instrumental works, but there with tasteful restraint.

Increasingly catchy, repetitive dance rhythms were being used. And there was an increase in Melody and Bass textures, usually in block chordal accompaniment. Opera had shown this accompaniment's viability during conversational sections (Recitatives). And there were advances in formal processes. A rhythmic motive would be used at the start of a piece, and it would be artfully repeated throughout the piece, as the chords changed. The motive itself would establish some sort of mood or state of mind, and those motives were regarded as "affections." Single Baroque Instrumental movements would invariably have a single affection, thus a single repeated motive. In that sense typical Baroque single movements were not internally dramatic. Drama, for Baroque composers, would be achieved when small groups, or soloists alternated with larger groups, such as is found in concertos of that time. (It would remain for later generations of composers in the late 1700s to go farther by having two somewhat different musical ideas juxtaposed within movements.) So by 1699 startling the opera audience with radical sudden change was fair game, and it would be somewhat so in Instrumental Music. The most dramatic effect would be in scores for enormously sized choirs and instruments alternating with solo singers, thus giving rise to the term, Colossal Baroque.

Throughout 1650 to 1700 the V – I sound was gradually gaining ground. By the end of the century the use of dissonance would eventually take a step in the direction of contextual acceptability. The V could easily have a 7 above the bass. And it would not be long before the V7 was treated as if it were a consonant sonority. Even the possible tritone was eventually heard as permissible, provided the resolution was to what would sound to us like a I. Also, by the end of the 1600s familiar chordal progressions were being repeated and easily perceived, thereby making a tonic seem all the more convincing. By 1700 a major/minor system was in place, with a growing vocabulary of fixed progressions. This, in time, would be referred to as "Tonality," and, with some notable emendations, it would remain in practice until the late 1800s.

OTHER INNOVATIONS

The years 1650 to 1700 would see many advances. All of the following were somehow governed by figured bass (Bass lines with numbers above the staff indicating desired chords).

There would sometimes be phrase--length (repeating) ostinatos in movements. The phrase length unit could be a returning melodic strand, or a repeating chordal progression. (Passacaglia, Chaconne) (Isorhythm returns, altered and disguised?)

There would be early examples of Fugue, as it is later known. Labels were in a state of transition. There would be an increase in juxtaposing the single player or small ensemble sound against a modestly large ensemble's. (Concerto effect) That was indeed dramatic.

There was an increase in Variation pieces, usually involving the "chattery--sounding" harpsichord. There would be multi--movement sets of pieces, later to be called Suites.

There would also be solo, duo, and trio non--vocal multi--movement pieces expediently called Sonatas. The use of the word Sonata assured all interested parties that it was indeed Instrumental Music.

And since figured bass seemed to govern all music, there would be a standing invitation for as much improvisation as was possible while observing the harmony controlling "figures." The best block chord performers were able to improvise separate lines while moving through the chords.

ITALIAN OPERA DOMINATES MOST OF EUROPE 1650 – 1700 (and beyond)

In the late l600s Italian opera was the vogue in all the courts of Europe. Even the insular, affluent, "culturally superior" Court of Louis 14 was not immune. The seemingly French Jean--Baptiste Lully (l632 – l637) was originally Italian, and he eventually combined Italian musical mannerisms with French staid formalisms to create the "French Lully sound." It was the duty of such music to honor that most formal and formidable of all monarchs. Even ballet of a curious type was included. Ballet would remain a feature of French opera in the coming centuries. Even if the "Lully sound" did not entirely match what the Italians were doing back home, in time more and more Italian features would find their way into French opera.

For readers interested in Opera, this semi--musical stage medium, other Italian composers who achieved the most were Agostini, Sartorio, Legranzi, Provenzole, Stradella, Pallavicini, Steffani, A. Scarlatti and Lotti. The various kinds of arias they used would eventually, to the extent possible, be imitated in Instrumental Music.

Lully's "French" approach to music was deemed by many of his international contemporaries worthy of imitation. Perhaps Lully had even invented the Instrumental Dance Suite, which was in turn emulated by many others, including J. S. Bach. It was the vogue. What happened in the French court was the fashion of the day. Certainly the Lully approach to opera overtures, in the hands of others, became "The French Ouverture." It was a standard pattern (slow – fast – slow), showing up even in contemporaneous English music. The Germans, on the other hand, observed and imitated both Lully and authentic Italian opera in detached wonderment.

Cantatas and Oratorios, regardless of composer or country, were really spin--offs of Italian opera, and they, too, became the vogue. The German Lutherans could easily adapt the Italian Cantata to their church music needs. In England Purcell emerged at the end of the Puritanical turmoil, and mimicked the practices on the continent. However, his music could still be remarkably original. He and John Blow revealed an inventiveness that for a while enlivened the English music of the day. Over in Vienna the church music of Johann Fux in his motets was adamantly attempting to recapture the Palestrina sound.

Lutheran music was making giant strides in this period, and that would continue beyond 1700. Chorales and various approaches to them were typical. There would be the opera-- influenced cantatas and occasional large scale works such as the likewise opera--influenced Passion and Oratorio. Some famous instrumental music composers at this time were Buxtehude, Pachelbel, and Neumeister.

YET MORE INNOVATIONS l650 -- 1700

The Germans improved the organ, and composers there added to that instrument's repertory. There were written pieces that gave the impression of artful improvisation. Sections of imitative counterpoint could alternate with dazzlingly fast passages.

The Fugue was born, having been an offspring of the earlier Ricercare. (Ricercares were originally organ versions of dignified choral works.) But the Fugue could be more animated, and certainly more unified by recycling a fixed motive. The Fugue would also employ the increasingly accepted chord progressions (V--I and others) that made the tonic obvious. In other words the Fugue in the hands of some composers would use the newly developed language of Tonality. But still, during this fifty--year period, harmonic progressions in the hands of others could be static or random, so long as a fixed motive was heard. Compared to the later Fugues of J.S. Bach, theirs could be frustratingly short, ending after they had just begun.

Equal temperament tuning was known and sometimes necessary. Equal temperament tuned all the intervals in the octave, so as to distribute slightly out--of--tune perfect fifths equally. As music become increasingly chromatic, and as modulations to other keys were used, the old tuning method, employing perfectly tuned 5ths, would fail on a complete keyboard as being "out of tune." However, there would always be die--hards who stayed with old tuning, and compliant diatonic repertory.

Much was being innovated. Lutheran composers were developing various ways of interpreting Chorales. Keyboard composers all over Western Europe were creating new types of pieces, such as sets of variations and suites (under various names). German composers had settled on a fixed form for the Suite. It began with a duple meter Allemande, followed by a triple meter Courante, then a slow triple meter Sarabande, and closing with a 6/8 Gigue. All of the movements were in Binary form, a favorite of most Baroque composers. Other kinds of dances and formal types could be interspersed.

To Baroque composers the word Sonata merely meant that it was a "sound" piece that did not involve singing. Therefore an ensemble could play a "Sonata." (Modern thinking is that a Sonata implies solo of one sort or another, but it was not always so.) Ensembles, consisting mostly of stringed instruments, would therefore present Sonatas. It would not be long before string sets of pieces, name intact, would be transferred to the keyboard, joining other pieces that had already been using that appellation.

This period saw the ascendency of the violin, along with specialists who played and taught its technique. It all started in Italy, the home and time of the great violin makers. (Stradivarius, Amati, etc.) It would therefore be natural for outstanding violin music to have its start in Italy.

The Trio Sonata always involved two violins playing separate lines, along with one or more bass line players and a keyboardist who read the figured bass. Such a "trio" could easily be expanded into a fledgling orchestra by increasing the number of players on the top lines, thereby creating violin sections. The number of players on the harmony instruments, as well as the instruments playing the bass line could also be increased. Here we have the first appearance of an orchestra, with a ready waiting substantial repertory that was originally intended for four players. In terms of instrumentation, this would easily be the first step towards the Sinfonia. This is probably how the Sinfonia first came about as it became part of opera.

In the latter 1600s the Concerto also came into being, and it would remain a fixture in the coming century, and beyond. For Baroque composers there were three types: 1.) a small group alternating with a large (grosso), 2.) a solo instrument alternating with a large group, and 3.) various sections of an orchestra alternating with one another. While Arcangelo Corelli is justifiably renowned for his handling of the violin, and as the creator of String orchestra concertos, it is his exact contemporary Giuseppe Torelli who perfected the Concerto single--movement Ritornello form, vaguely resembling a Rondo form. His innovations would remain fixed for other composers in the coming 1700s. Assuming he was working with the first type of Concerto described above, he showed where the returning idea (the large group ritornello) should be placed, where the small group interjections should be placed, and what the key relationships worked and how other procedures should be used.

It could be said that all that was achieved in the period 1650 to 1700, more than set the stage for the momentous achievements of the Bach/Handel/Vivaldi/Rameau period that was to follow.

1699: THE SITUATION

The Italians were perfecting Ensemble Music called Sonatas. Those Sonatas, in turn, would be imitated in other countries, especially in Germany. The Germans, such as Froberger, Pachelbel, JKF Fischer and Kuhnau, sometimes using other labels, would add to their "Suites" musical elements that blended Italian procedures with features more native to their sensibilities. Kuhnau, especially, transferred Instrumental Music procedures to his keyboard Sonatas. Orchestral Suites, keyboard reductions or not, were flourishing in Germany for about the first half of the 1700s. Most German composers, especially J. Sebastian Bach, were, or were about to try their hand at this medium.

The Italians were exploiting violins in groups to show what was possible. The string orchestral works of Corelli and Torelli were in full force, demonstrating violin techniques and, in the case of Torelli, formal procedures. Ordinarily all movements would be in the same key. It may have been Corelli who established the practice of placing the slow movement in a closely related key. In terms of small groups of instruments and multi--movement pieces, there emerged two types of Suites intended for two violin lines, sometimes just one, and continuo (bass line instruments and a single keyboard observing the figured bass numbers above their bass clef lines): the Church Sonata and the Chamber (Reception Room) Sonata. Both types of movement groupings could include separate pieces from the other's usual offerings. In time the dance type movements were so melodically elaborate that an actual dancer's need for clearly heard beats was either blurred or ignored. Other outstanding Italian composers of sonatas for string groups were Legrenzi, Cazzati, Vitali, and Bassani.

1600 – 1750 J. SEBASTIAN BACH See Layer I for J. S. Bach information.

In 1700 J. S. Bach was 15 and considering paid employment. Beginning in 1708 he started out as an organist in various churches, and remained so occupied for about five years, until age 22. It was then that his early organ works were created. Next he worked at Weimar for about nine years, and while there he probably ink--copied (hence analyzed) the string works of Vivaldi and other "top" names of his day. He could not have failed to notice the weak harmonic element that was so typical of these highly respected works. Then for six years he was the Music Director at Coethen, a position he held until he was about 38. It was at Coethen that he composed much of his purely instrumental Music. Then at 38 he became the chief city musician at the important Lutheran church in Leipzig. He held that position until his death. It was there he produced the bulk of his choral and vocal music, most of it for the Lutheran Church. There were also scores for other purposes.

A few of Bach's contemporaries who excelled in German Church Music were Graupner, Mattheson, and Telemann. Each had secured lucrative positions. These and a number of others would all occasionally try their hand at opera, but to limited success. The most famous of Bach's contemporaries were Vivaldi, Rameau and Handel, all of whom eventually enjoyed immense fame and success.

VIVALDI

Antonio Vivaldi (1678 – 1741) was vastly prolific, famous and successful throughout Bach's life. There is an enormous accumulation of scores, many of which are purely Instrumental. One music historian racked up 450 concertos, 300 of which involve a solo instrument. After the 1950s a number of concerned opera fans and scholars longed for some contact with Vivaldi's nearly 50 operas. So far, limited contact has not proven positive.

His is a glib Instrumental style that evidently still pleases many listeners in the modern world. An early 21st Century poll of London music critics (as reported in the BBC Music Magazine) had the majority voting Vivaldi the most boring of composers to review. Even if that is the case, and since his scores were given much attention in their day, his innovations should be given some attention. Evidently his clearly stated themes were exemplary. His incessant, almost mechanical rhythms were widely imitated. So was the importance he placed on the concerto's middle slow movement. Later pre--Mozart symphonies and concertos benefitted from his Sinfonia and Concerto models. However, if Vivaldi went too far in his sequential patterning, later composers were careful to do so in moderation. Other features such as the importance of the bass line, block--chordal accompaniment, and restriction to the primary triads (I – IV and V), sometimes attributed to him, were typical of music by contemporary and succeeding composers and would have come about irrespective of Vivaldi's use or non--use.

RAMEAU

The scores of Jean--Philippe Rameau (1683 – 1764) must be considered apart from his highly significant contributions to Music Theory. Aside from some keyboard collections, he was basically an opera composer. Though there are no "stand--alone" Instrumental scores, there are a number of Instrumental dance suites and passages in his operas that can be programmed on symphonic programs. In the 21st Century more and more of his operas have become available on compact disks, thus making possible an assessment of his compositional skill. His music is unique, thus assuring his position in Music History. While his operas conform to the stilted requirements of French Opera at the time, his handling of harmony makes his music more vital than that of his predecessor Lully. In fact some scenes in certain operas are so taut with intensity and excitement, that one knows this is a major composer.

Oddly, while Bach's creative career was in its last 15 years, Rameau's was just heating up. Though Rameau was only two years older than Bach, his creative career would continue some fourteen years beyond the death of his important contemporary. A few generalizations are possible in comparing the work of the two. While J. Sebastian Bach luxuriated in contrapuntal textures, Rameau stayed with a more easily comprehended melody with block--chordal accompaniment. Bach's exploitation of harmony is well beyond that of Rameau's. However, Rameau's Theoretical pronouncements help to clarify and validate the more complex progressions and modulations of Bach. On basic matters each agreed with one another without knowing it. Rameau, using his own limited chordal pallet, wanted the harmony to be very simple with occasional modulations. He relied for the most part on the basic triads (I, IV, V) at any given moment. Rameau knew that his chordal progressions sounded "right," and it seems he spent most of his Theoretical time trying to prove that they were scientifically/acoustically natural. His orchestration is unique in its prominent use of oboes and other double reed instruments. With that and his other basic traits, it is not hard to recognize a Rameau "sound" during a brief unnamed encounter.

HANDEL

George Frederick Handel (1685 – 1759) may have been the most famous and successful composer in his day, if success in London is considered the top of possible achievements. Though born in Germany, for a while he lived and composed in Italy, absorbing as much of the ways of Italian opera as was possible. Then at the age of 30 in 1710 he secured a position back in Germany at the court of Hanover. This was fortuitous because the monarch (Prince Elector) there would become George I of England four years later. Handel, already having spent two leaves trying his wings in London, would follow his monarch to London, and would begin a nearly four--decade career of successes. There would of course be downturns and setbacks, but overall he was a success.

In time he created, and sometimes even produced a number of Italian language operas, the London fashion of which would only be temporary since most people there did not understand the language. So, beginning in the 1730s, he turned his attention mostly to Oratorios. (Religious operas with no costumes, scenery and little stage movement.) His Oratorios would use the English language. It could not have been a better move since his adopted country was beginning a long--standing choral tradition. Eventually Handel would permanently endear himself to the British nation because of his 26 Oratorios.

Though Handel's main focus was choral and vocal music, he did produce a number of respected instrumental works. (Concertos, solo Sonatas, Trio Sonatas, and his famous Water and Fireworks Suites.) He was a practical and speedy composer, and did not hesitate to recycle earlier works. In one instance he stole from another composer. If one listens closely to his Instrumental music, one might hear recurring formulas. His was a life of compositional deadlines, and speed mattered. On the whole, all his Instrumental scores sound vibrant and engaging, thus helping to explain his continuing success with listeners.

1750: THE SITUATION

Musical tastes were changing fast. It seems that all the courts and cities of Europe were accepting styles of music from all other European locations. The most rapid changes may have been due to the rise of the Merchant Class, both owners and employees, people who by this time were increasingly important and knowledgeable, and their tastes were being taken into account. Since public concerts were increasing, ordinary people connected with businesses began populating the audiences, and they would ultimately control the direction music would take. Often they could purchase printed music, and Merchant--Owners of various businesses could pay for music to their tastes. And if they were amateur musicians, they could determine what music would sell. That base of public wanted pleasant, pleasing music. More and more concerts were open to a burgeoning public, and composers sought to address it.

Already in the l720s new musical styles had come into being and were part of the 1750 picture. The older Baroque way of creating music was still around, but increasingly out of favor. Concertos were still being created, but a new medium, the multi--movement Symphony, was being heard. Over in Spain keyboardist Domenico Scarlatti, was seemingly experimenting with all sorts of new devices in his piano pieces. That change was in the air can be seen in his scores. Certainly melody and an accompaniment of slightly varied block chords was now the preferred texture everywhere, and it would remain so for many decades. Other keyboard music, especially in Italian cultural centers and in Paris, was increasingly popular and featured uncomplicated, and sometimes overly sentimental melodies accompanied by simplistic left--hand accompaniments. The basic triads (I, IV and V) were arpeggiated in left--hand eighth--note patterns that we now call Alberti Bass. Chords changed at a medium--to--slow rate of speed.

A certain kind of keyboard music, the type created by Francois Couperin, was on its way out. It involved right hand "melodies" that were so overly decorous, the underlying melody, if there was one, could barely be perceived. Another newer kind of music, not just for keyboard, was sometimes seeking to express personal kinds of emotions, and at other times giving martial fanfares, no doubt imitating what could be heard in operas. Such fanfares found their way into Symphonias. When it came to creating symphonias and music for any smaller combination, composers were using just the basic triads. (Was it just a coincidence that at this time Rameau's Theoretical writings, stressing the importance of primary triads, had become primary reading material?) Modulations were used, but only moderately. This was the accepted way to compose for a number of coming decades.

Another innovation that seemed to be in place at mid--century was the notion that an instrumental movement need not recycle one small motive throughout its entire length. What could be more dramatic than having a secondary idea or theme enter after the primary idea or theme has established itself at the beginning. A single movement could then have the two in alternating temporal opposition, eventually being somehow reconciled near

51

the movement's end. The first musical idea, could be "answered" or followed by a balancing idea in (usually) the Dominant key. These approaches were indeed somewhat dramatic.

It was also around the middle of the century that another procedure established itself: periodicity. Musical "sentencing" could be symmetric in that an idea of two measures length would be followed by another of two measures, and they in turn fit into four measures. Two four-measure length ideas would fit into eight, two eights into sixteen, two sixteen into thirty-two, and so-forth. Such symmetric phrasing, though not always present, would pervade music for at least a century and a half. And it was not only matching lengths that mattered. A unit, be it a motive, phrase, section, movement, etc., was stated and then followed by a balancing counter statement (In the "answering" sense mentioned above). How does such and such a unit balance and complement what had preceded it? Decorations, mainly played by the violins, would still be present, but vastly reduced. The harpsichord, mainstay of the earlier era and used for holding things together harmonically, was gradually being phased out.

Whereas earlier Baroque composers favored Binary form, by 1750 there were attempts to breathe new life into it. Since the new looser phrasing involving a wide variety of pitch lengths, it would be easy and would open the door to new possibilities not previously possible in the Baroque discipline. Multi-movement symphonies, or early vestiges of a sort, were appearing that resembled that of the coming Mozart era. Those symphonies would display the new "altered" Binary forms by having a small central section (that later became the Development). There were also exciting demonstrations of new orchestration and the play of juxtaposed loud/soft changes.

Ironically, some of the newest trends were exhibited in scores by composers whose primary talent was producing otherwise routine scores. This transitional period is over-supplied with music that is correct in form and procedure, but having no redeeming spark. Themes and ideas were in the right places, but they lacked inherent spirit. However, the stage was set for the appearance of a genius who would combine these elements in works of timeless beauty.

1750 – 1800 MOZART

Though he was born a little after 1750, and died before 1800, his importance is so great that he dominates this half-century.

(See Layer I for the Mozart summation.)

HAYDN

Franz Josef Haydn seems to have assimilated and demonstrated the best of the new trends taking shape by 1750. In time he amassed a large, imaginative and highly original catalog of works. It was ten or so years before his first scores appeared in the l760s. His earliest piano sonatas serve as an example of the newer freedoms. From measure to measure the wider range of single note durations would never have been accepted in the old Baroque mindset. The music is tuneful, and frequently demonstrates Alberti Bass accompaniments. The forms are binary, taking the listener to the Dominant (V) key, just as the Baroque composers would have, but the very mood seems to be one of enjoyment in the keyboard's possibilities, rather than the consistent, almost cerebral rigidity so often in typical Baroque scores. In Haydn there is much periodicity, as described above. Supposedly Haydn said that the piano scores of (J.P.) Emanuel Bach were a major influence. However, to the modern inquirer, the connection remains elusive in connecting the works of these two composers. Maybe it is just vibrant genius that separates the two, present in Haydn and absent in Emanuel Bach.

Haydn, throughout his long life, would continue creating happy, sunny scores. Any pieces that stray into darker emotions (minor keys and somber leanings) were probably the result of a temporary fashion of the times. Aside from the happy/sunny aspect, his output is remarkably neutral in mood. In his single--movement sonata forms, the second theme or thematic area never strays from the same emotion stated in the first theme. In fact it can easily be a variation of Theme I. The tunes and the processes he puts them through were and remain musically satisfying, testifying to his continued success on concert stages. In his day his many followers were probably amazed at his continued originality. It would be hard to find instances where a Haydn score recycled the sounds of any of his contemporaries.

Haydn's chief forms were those used by Mozart. Mozart may have indeed used Haydn models as a point of departure. Often Haydn's forms themselves would be creatively adapted. An example might be the so--called Double Variations, a set of Variations with two alternating themes.

1800 – 1825 Beethoven/Napoleon

Beethoven adopted the classic forms used by Mozart and Haydn, expanding and extending their overall length. He also extended ending codas, so that, on occasion, their length rivals the other sections in a particular movement. His is an intense and (for the day) over--emotional approach to music. He dared to exaggerate. What he created pleased the average listener who needed more repetition, and obvious extreme articulations in order to grasp and appreciate a musical process. While it is possible to go along with the notion that both Beethoven and Napoleon were, each in their own way, revolutionaries, and that they suited the times, one should not imagine that the one who was responsible for so many deaths and political disruption is to be equated with a creator of timeless beauty.

Readers of Music History often confuse handicaps and situations in Beethoven's life with his actual music. Whatever hindrances he may, and in certain instances, did have are superfluous to the created actual music. The music is outstanding because of his talent, and not because of his life-- situation.

SCHUBERT

Franz Schubert's short life (31 years) was spent creating score after score. The Vienna of his day had many young, aspiring composers, and Schubert could easily have been "lost in the crowd," and indeed he was! It took decades after his death before the European music establishment realized the worth of his music. He was also remarkably good at the few operas he created, but recognition for that achievement would take far more than a century.

1825 – 1850 PIANO IS KING

Aside from Mozart's 20, and Beethoven's 30 preeminent Sonatas created decades earlier, this period has to be the Golden Age of Piano composition, especially from Chopin's standpoint. Much future piano music beyond 1850 will be in reaction to Chopin's body of work. To composers, the piano was its own "symphony orchestra." A whole world of possibilities presented itself.

Here is a brief summary of the momentous music for piano created in this period:

Chopin: A book of Preludes, a book of *Etudes*, a book of *Polonaises*, four *Ballades*, four *Impromptus*, four *Scherzos*, three multi--movement *Sonatas*, *Barcarolle*, *Bolero*, *Berceuse*, *Tarantella*, *Phantasie* and two *Piano Concertos*.

Schumann: *Abegg Variations*, Papillons, Davidsbundler *Dances*, *Toccata*, *Carnaval*, Kriesleriana, three multi--movement *Sonatas*, *Faschingschwank of Vienna*, *Arabesque*, various collections and a *Piano Concerto*.

Mendelssohn: *Songs Without Words,* specialty pieces and two *Piano Concertos.*

Franz Liszt: Most of his piano works, often having shimmery, stunning surface qualities.

Of course, other kinds of music were being created. Schumann created four symphonies that almost succeed in continuing the tradition of the Beethoven nine. Mendelssohn created five Symphonies and various depictive orchestral pieces, as well as two Oratorios. Hector Berlioz was composing and conducting his succession of excellently orchestrated, rhythmically exciting, highly dramatic free-- style symphonies and depictive pieces. (Free--style because, while melody is admirably presented, acoustically influenced harmonic progression is either absent or entirely ignored.)

Most of the above composers, except Chopin, created choral works, most of which is of little importance. However, Mendelssohn's oratorios survive as important staples, as do his Chamber works. Schumann created a whole body of Art Songs, as well as some significant Chamber works. In his Art Songs, Schumann felt he was continuing the tradition started by Franz Schubert, but with the piano part on a much higher status. Liszt did, or attempted to do what the above three composers were doing.

Opera, ever since the 1820s. was moving in its separate course of development with many productions. Some were outstanding, but most were transient. (21ˢᵗ Century opera companies are producing many of the transient operas in order to reassess.) A good history of opera will give all the prominent names of composers, librettists and productions. During this period of intense opera activity, instrumental music would continue to grow and develop on its own, sometimes influenced by what was heard coming out of the opera orchestra pit. Some examples would be new instruments such as the improved harp and valved brass instruments.

1850 – 1900 BRAHMS

Nearly all of Brahms' orchestral works are important, and continue to remain in the preferred Symphonic Repertory. There are Four *Symphonies*, two early *Serenades*, two *Piano Concertos*, a *Violin Concerto*, a *Double Concerto* for violin and cello, *Variations on a Theme by Haydn*, *Academic Festival Overture*, and a so--called *Tragic Overture*. There are also twenty--four chamber works, 250 Art and Folk songs, and a number of important Choral works. His Piano works would be equally and deservedly as important as his other works were it not for some questionable occasional poor piano formatting (What and how much each hand plays, as well as needlessly complex notation). The pianist who overcomes those problems will experience the well established Brahms excellence.

During this "Brahms period" much other music of importance was being composed. Belgian Cesar Franck, in addition to his innovative organ works, created at least four lasting Chamber works as well as his unique D minor Symphony and some depiction pieces for orchestra. Gabriel Faure was creating his Chamber works, as well as the beginning succession of his highly valued Art Songs. Georges Bizet and Charles Gounod, seemingly engulfed in Opera, both created a few Symphonies. Also Camille Saint Saens was creating a succession of works for all manner of media that stressed a practical approach to music.

A few composers of importance resided in European countries that were either seeking independence, or national assertion. Those composers created music indigenous to their locale or national spirit. Smetana, Dvorak, and Rimsky Korsakov, and the Norwegian Edvard Grieg all created scores that were attracting world--wide audiences. A new sense of Musical Internationalism seemed to be taking hold.

In the German speaking portions of Europe there were highly important developments. Young Richard Strauss was creating a succession of orchestral pieces that were described in Layer I. The first of the Mahler symphonies was also alluded to in Layer I. Hugo Wolf was creating an entire catalog of Art Songs that continued the tradition of Schubert. Anton Bruckner was creating a string of eight symphonies that utilized Wagnerian operatic tonal/orchestral language. They are stark and unique, even while sometimes seeming studied and forced.

Abstract orchestral music was also coming from an unexpected source: Richard Wagner. Even though he devoted his life to his "Music Drama" operas, and even though his operatic Preludes and Interludes had contextual plot connections, a number these pieces were accepted and fit nicely into the world of abstract music. The non--operatic world of music could not but help notice the musical brilliance of a mind otherwise consumed with myth--plots, and imaginary metaphysical symbols.

There were other glimmers of music and careers that began late in this period, but properly belong in the next multi--decade continuance.

1900 – 1930 DEBUSSY and RAVEL

Other highly significant activity during this time period:

A veritable explosion in concert/recital music had been taking place, as well as that in the separate medium of opera. This abundance had been accelerating since the late 1880s. As the 1900s began Richard Strauss and Gustave Mahler would be creating their final Symphonies; Scriabin would create his remarkably unique *Poem of Ecstasy* for orchestra; Rachmaninoff would pace over several decades the creation of his 2nd and 3rd Symphonies, as well as his 2nd through 4th Piano Concertos; Jean Sibelius would likewise pace his 2nd through 7th Symphonies; Edward Elgar would try to match the excitement created by his 1899 *Enigma Variations* for Orchestra with a string of works that never quite matched the earlier work; Ralph Vaughan Williams, using his own relaxed tonal language, would create the first three in his succession of Symphonies; Gustav Holst in 1918 would create his ever--living *Planets* for orchestra; Gabriel Faure in his old age would create three more chamber works and continuum of his of Art Songs, Erik Satie would inspire and encourage a number of young French composers to explore casual and flippant musical language as a means of validity in their works; and Ottorino Respighi would create most of his giant and impressive statements for orchestra that painted the history of his beloved Rome.

And intervening, almost in the middle of this thirty--year period would be four years of war that ripped apart European culture. Resolute composers, showing their contempt for a civilization gone awry, continued to the best of their ability while denying mass insanity was taking place. (Composers have always been cultural builders in spite of possibly horrible conditions.) This was a period when many in Society--at--large felt cultural and political revolution were in the air. Small pockets of enthusiastic participants, as well as some individuals were inventing, exploring and demonstrating/performing new methods of tonal expression, probably in tandem with the new expressions seen in the Plastic Arts of the time. Bartok in Hungary was combining notes in new dissonant ways. Later he would create the first four of his ever--living String Quartets; Schoenberg was involved in his unique activities (described in Layer I), Anton Webern (a Schoenberg student) was expressing himself in a brevity and concentrated pitch--use hitherto unexplored; Berg (also a Schoenberg student) was combining the old with the new, Charles Ives in America was innovating all sorts of new sounds and procedures for large ensembles; a group in Italy (around 1914) was exploring expressivity with noises, and Lev/Leon Termin in Russia in 1919 was inventing an electronic instrument (the Theremin) that is played without being touched. There were many others, who in their own way, either rejoiced in the new age, or rebelled against the past, and wanted their name associated new ways. Aaron Copland (in the '20s) was contriving dissonant orchestral works that would be more respected than performed or accepted. And beginning in 1924 a seemingly solitary figure, 26--year--old George Gershwin, innovated a new kind of concert music that combined French harmony with popular theater melodies and street rhythms. General audiences were thrilled. Though many at the time called what he had created Jazz, in reality the Gershwin orchestral works, attractive as they are, would never quite fit into either the improvisatory Jazz world or that of Symphonic/Concert/Recital music.

1930 – 1950 BARTOK/STRAVINSKY/HINDEMITH

Other highly significant achievements during this time period:

During these years a number of composers from a number of world countries emerged. Often they gained fame through the success of just one work. At other times they were associated with a particular country and symbolized an almost localized national fervor. That, however, did not prevent performances of their works in foreign countries. Nationalism was seen as an attractive element on orchestral programs everywhere. Music in Germany would undergo a necessary redefinition because so much of its identity was repressed under Hitler. By 1950, under new thinking, it was roaring back to life.

NATIONALISTIC FIGURES

England had William Walton and a young Benjamin Britten; Brazil had Heitor Villa – Lobos; Mexico had Carlos Chavez; and France had Honegger, Milhaud and Poulenc (though these Frenchmen might have denied their music was nationalistic in any way). Russia had Prokofiev (having returned to Russia after a two--decade stint in the West), Shostakovich, Kabalevsky, and Khachaturian, all producing under soviet (committee) surveillance. Other countries were producing composers of more limited fame.

A number of composers emerged in the United States. Aaron Copland would happen upon a distinctly American type of music in his ballets and film scores. In addition to Copland there were Charles Ives (newly resurrected in the twilight of his years), Walter Piston, Roger Sessions, Howard Hanson, Roy Harris, William Schuman, Samuel Barber, Leonard Bernstein, and a young Elliot Carter. Even what George Gershwin was creating counts as nationalistic. (To Europeans, unfortunately, it seemed as if every American score after 1924 that utilized a fast steady beat was regarded as jazz.) United States Orchestras were sampling the scores of these newcomers, and sometimes scores were commercially recorded for added beneficial scrutiny.

Composers of nationalistic music often produced a music that could be more easily grasped by ordinary citizens, while exhibiting musical turns and phrases that recalled folk or street--level music. Predictably the forms had to be more extensive. The appeal to ordinary citizens was true of, among others, Spanish and Portuguese culture nations, as well as the United States. Sometimes nationalistic composers produced a music the traits of which are unique, not easily simplified and exist more by association, than by obvious folksong connections.

WELL OUT OF THE ORDINARY

Another development was the appearance individuals who wrote music that questioned the very essence of what music really is, or should be. Chief among them were Henry Cowell, and a young John Cage.

1950 – 1970 Elliot Carter, Roberto Gerhard and Composition Contests

Refer to Layer I for information on Carter and Gerhard.

12 TONE SERIALISTS

Some composers, perhaps beginning in the 1950s or slightly earlier, in their estimation, were being very modern by creating Twelve--tone works. It certainly was fashionable during the '50s when Modernism seemed to be the way of the future. A number of works were created that sought to be either close, or far away from the supposedly older ways of "Tonality." Some scores were even, in their own way, remarkably beautiful (and remain so). But perhaps too many composers, often associated with universities, were stepping up to claim fame. Some were even imitating the music of Anton Webern, believing that his intensely abbreviated music showed the way of the future. (The many score imitations of Webern led to many a short elegant score.) However, performances of such music came and went, with no lasting effect. What was missing was sufficient audience support. Maybe the serial achievements of Schoenberg, Berg and Webern, as well as their associates, were a phenomenon of their particular 20th--Century period, forever locked in a time--frame previous to 1950. By the 1950s such serialism was thirty years old, and any more of such scores might seem to some to be anachronistic. The rush towards Schoenberg or Webern--type serialism would fade during the next few decades, of course after a number of remarkable scores had been written.

Beginning in the 1950s any kind of High Art was having trouble co--existing with an ever burgeoning, ever distracting Popular Culture. Would sincere statements of High Art even be noticed, let alone appreciated. Popular music, through mass media, had become so ubiquitous and powerful that the designation "Art Music" becomes necessary. Even the term "Classic Music" began to be used by powerful pop music conglomerates as an all--encompassing term to describe any kind of concert/recital music.

KINDS OF MUSIC

What Henry Cowell, John Cage and others had begun in earlier decades continued in full force in these decades. Musical experiences in their view should include all manner of stimuli. Art Music itself was becoming pluralistic (in every conceivable way).

It was in the 1960s that Improvisational (small) Groups came along. What they produced was certainly group composition, rather than the product of a single mind. It also qualifies as Existentialistic in that music was created for the moment, and not to be preserved in any way, other than for recordings. One exponent called it "playing at music," rather than actually playing it. Maybe that was true.

One procedure, or perhaps a sound or effect to be pursued, was that of Stasis (non--movement). A sound, be it a chord, melodic turn or rhythm, was to be repeated artistically, with only the subtlest form of variation. Stravinsky in his *Rite of Spring* had presaged this with his static "time--blocks" having even--beat momentum and returning unpredictably throughout the piece. But the newer kind of stasis manipulation would reject steady beats, or perceptible beats of any kind. Edgar Varese may well be the chief exponent of this approach. While he had been doing this for some decades, it is only after 1960 that his efforts were noticed.

Another kind of music was espoused and demonstrated by Roger Sessions, although he was undoubtedly acting intuitively, unaware of espousing anything. (His short books make for interesting reading.) His was the "Emotional Journey" score. The ideal medium was the Symphony Orchestra, the language was highly chromatic (duodecuple), but short of actual serialism. The texture was often as thick as possible with one layer or line transpiring simultaneously with one or several others with an attempt at distortion. The probable hope of the composer was to create something the listener had never heard before, and the total effect should be as if emotional waves in succession were washing over the listener. Any moods or states of mind the listener experiences should be positively individualized. Whatever strange, extreme or unknown reactions the listener went through were regarded as acceptable. Roger Sessions perfected this type of orchestral score over the course of some forty years and nine symphonies. It may be that Elliot Carter's scores achieved the same effect, whatever the intention. Carter seems to have been luxuriating in the joy of intensely rational procedures.

COMPOSITION CONTESTS

There probably had been prizes offered for outstanding compositions in the mid to latter l800s. Certainly there were in the United States after 1900. By the 1920s there were a few high--profile contests, among them the highest profile was the Pulitzer Prize. The Pulitzer Prize is basically a newspaper prize. The music prize has always been presided over by Columbia University faculty. To win a Pulitzer Prize meant that the recipient would always be referred to in newspapers with "Pulitzer" before his name. Scanning the list of annual prize winners since the l920s one is tempted to see just where (American) music history was headed. Or, was that true? Some, if not most of the winning composers' names, along with their winning music, faded with time. Maybe such scores should be resurrected and performed. Certainlys the intentions of the contests were good, if not exactly prophetic.

There were Ford and Rockefeller Foundation awards, scholarships with a politician's name attached, residencies in European cultural locales, along with other occasionally independent high money prizes that got press coverage. Maybe it was only in America that such prizes and honors took on the aura of successful composition. After 1960 there was an increase of such competitions, often with lucrative prize money involved. After 1970 there were awards and commissions from the National Endowment for the Arts – an effort that would be questionable because of the excessive politics involved. Was most of the music then just ignored?

Problems and questions arise. Do prizes represent any lasting achievement in the History of Music? Do the prizes insure the perpetuation of the prize giver's name, rather than that of the winner? Would any prize insure that a winning work would be accepted and performed in the future? Were such contests and prizes a poor substitute for national interest in serious Modern "Classical" music? Paul Hindemith in his book *A Composer's World*, questions whether prize and award winning is real success.

AFTER 1970

Refer to pages 24 – 25.

At this point, the reader is referred to general Music History writings and textbooks, both new and old, each of which reflects unique perspectives on this fascinating subject.

Printed in the United States
By Bookmasters